STRATEGIC LEGAL RESEARCH

**Finding the Information You Need
Efficiently and Cost-Effectively**

Second Edition

ASPEN SELECT SERIES

STRATEGIC LEGAL RESEARCH

**Finding the Information You Need
Efficiently and Cost-Effectively**

Second Edition

Tobin A. Sparling
Professor of Law
South Texas College of Law

To contact Customer Service, e-mail
customer.service@wolterskluwer.com,
call 1-800-234-1660, fax 1-800-901-9075, or mail correspondence to:

   Wolters Kluwer
   Attn: Order Department
   PO Box 990
   Frederick, MD 21705

Printed in the United States of America.

1 2 3 4 5 6 7 8 9 0

ISBN 978-1-4548-6989-4

About Wolters Kluwer Law & Business

Wolters Kluwer Law & Business is a leading global provider of intelligent information and digital solutions for legal and business professionals in key specialty areas, and respected educational resources for professors and law students. Wolters Kluwer Law & Business connects legal and business professionals as well as those in the education market with timely, specialized authoritative content and information-enabled solutions to support success through productivity, accuracy and mobility.

Serving customers worldwide, Wolters Kluwer Law & Business products include those under the Aspen Publishers, CCH, Kluwer Law International, Loislaw, ftwilliam.com and MediRegs family of products.

CCH products have been a trusted resource since 1913, and are highly regarded resources for legal, securities, antitrust and trade regulation, government contracting, banking, pension, payroll, employment and labor, and healthcare reimbursement and compliance professionals.

Aspen Publishers products provide essential information to attorneys, business professionals and law students. Written by preeminent authorities, the product line offers analytical and practical information in a range of specialty practice areas from securities law and intellectual property to mergers and acquisitions and pension/benefits. Aspen's trusted legal education resources provide professors and students with high-quality, up-to-date and effective resources for successful instruction and study in all areas of the law.

Kluwer Law International products provide the global business community with reliable international legal information in English. Legal practitioners, corporate counsel and business executives around the world rely on Kluwer Law journals, looseleafs, books, and electronic products for comprehensive information in many areas of international legal practice.

Loislaw is a comprehensive online legal research product providing legal content to law firm practitioners of various specializations. Loislaw provides attorneys with the ability to quickly and efficiently find the necessary legal information they need, when and where they need it, by facilitating access to primary law as well as state-specific law, records, forms and treatises.

ftwilliam.com offers employee benefits professionals the highest quality plan documents (retirement, welfare and non-qualified) and government forms (5500/PBGC, 1099 and IRS) software at highly competitive prices.

MediRegs products provide integrated health care compliance content and software solutions for professionals in healthcare, higher education and life sciences, including professionals in accounting, law and consulting.

Wolters Kluwer Law & Business, a division of Wolters Kluwer, is headquartered in New York. Wolters Kluwer is a market-leading global information services company focused on professionals.

Dedication

To Sally J. Langston, who taught me to be a better legal researcher

and to

Michael Mistric and Maxine Goodman, for their unwavering support

Summary of Contents

Table of Contents

Chapter 1
The Goal of Legal Research

Legal research seeks to retrieve authoritative, relevant, and current legal and supporting materials that judges and attorneys require so they may ascertain how any given case fits within the context of the law and social policy.

I. Why Are Legal Research Skills So Important?

Proficiency in legal research ranks among the most valued skills in the legal profession. Knowledge of the law is essential to any legal practice. Indeed, there is scarcely any human activity that is not subject in some respect to legal rules and regulations. As the gatekeepers of the law, attorneys owe an obligation to their clients, the courts, and society in general to know what the law is and how it is applied. Quite simply, legal research is the mechanism through which this obligation is realized.

Nor does a practicing attorney's need for legal research ever end. The law is constantly changing. New statutory, regulatory, and judge-made (common) laws are constantly being enacted. Existing statutes may be modified or repealed. Judicial interpretations of existing statutory and common laws may change. Even the factual situations applicable to existing laws change as technology innovates and society evolves.

Legal research skills are also important in a purely practical sense. Skillful legal research saves time for attorneys and money for their clients. When the "best" law has been found, legal writing and drafting are made easier, legal arguments become more effective, and client advice can be given with greater assurance. Last but not least, if the very notion of legal research makes you cringe, good legal research skills are essential to getting it done quickly and effectively, so you can move on to something you find more enjoyable.

Chapter 2
Legal Research in the Practice of Law

Legal research does not take place in a vacuum. The expectations, which your employers place upon you as a legal researcher, will vary somewhat according to the nature of your place of practice. The expectations in various practice situations are summarized below. However, you would be wise to ascertain precisely what is expected of you in terms of legal research methodology whenever you enter into a new employment relationship.

I. Law Firm Practice

Although the practice of law is a profession, a law firm is a business that seeks to make a profit. Lawyers generally have an established hourly rate and clients are typically billed for every six minutes a lawyer is engaged with their cases. This includes time spent on consultations, legal research, legal writing, discovery, court appearances, and other work done on the client's behalf.

A law firm expects its attorneys to conduct themselves so the time spent on a client's case and any related costs are appropriate for the matter at hand in accordance with firm practice and the custom of the legal community. Put bluntly, a law firm does not want to expend $5000 of attorney research time and services on a $500 case. An expenditure of resources in excess of what can be billed to the client must be written off, resulting in a loss to firm revenues.

Clients, as consumers, also expect to receive value for the attorney fees they pay. Many are resistant to paying the high costs associated with some types of electronic legal research. Others cannot afford to pay such costs.

As an attorney engaged in legal research, you need to understand the costs in time and money associated with the legal research tools at your disposal. For example, although no user charges result when consulting traditional paper or free online resources, they may require longer expenditures of attorney time to get the information required. On the other hand, although fee-based electronic resources may facilitate the retrieval of information in a shorter time, high user costs often result, particularly if the researcher is unfamiliar with the area of law under investigation. Increasingly, firms have formal or informal policies concerning the use of different legal research tools. You should inquire whether any such exist whenever you begin work at a firm.

II. Legal Practice in Government

Although the profit motive is absent in government practice, the cost of legal research remains of critical concern, owing to requirements that government agencies not exceed their allocated budgets. Budgetary constraints may also restrict the range of legal research sources that are available. Electronic research tools, in particular, are often less prevalent in government than in law firm practice. Staff shortages may place a premium on efficient and effective legal research.

III. Legal Practice in the Business Setting

Although some legal departments (particularly of major corporations) boast an extensive range of legal research resources, this is more the exception than the rule. More likely, legal research tools will be restricted to those that are most commonly used in connection with the business of the company. The business world's concentration on cost-effectiveness and efficiency extends to corporate legal departments and will be expected when legal research is performed.

IV. Legal Practice in Nonprofit Organizations

Legal research resources in non-profit settings may be quite limited and often are restricted to those that relate directly to the focus of the organization. As in government practice, budgetary constraints and staffing shortages make cost-effective and efficient legal research an imperative. In nonprofit legal practice, it may be particularly critical to be aware of free, online research resources and of outside legal research collections, such as law school libraries, which grant access to nonaffiliated members of the general public.

Chapter 3
Overview of the
Research Process

This section presents the outline of a strategy for efficient and cost-effective legal research that gets results. The successive steps will be discussed at greater length in the sections that follow. One core principle underlying this strategy is the proposition that thinking should always precede action. The skilled researcher thinks about the facts of the case in relation to the legal question and the potential keywords that follow from the facts and the issue. He or she then thinks about the jurisdiction and about what legal resources allow him or her to benefit most from the prior research of others. All of this thinking should have occurred before the researcher even sets foot in the law library or logs on to an electronic search tool on the computer.

Of course, electronic research resources win hands down over paper resources in terms of the quickness and ease of document retrieval. The downside, however, is that many of the most comprehensive electronic resources, such as Lexis and Westlaw, can be quite expensive to use. Thus, a second core principle underlying this research strategy is the recognition that an appropriate balance must be struck between cost-saving and time-saving. Fortunately, this is a lot easier to accomplish than one might initially think.

Secondary sources are books that discuss the law. Although they do not comprise the law, itself, and generally are not cited as one's chief authority in legal documents, they serve several important functions. First, secondary sources are available in formats, both paper and electronic, which require no payment for user access. Secondly, these sources are very user-friendly in that their finding tools, such as keyword subject indexes, are geared toward researchers who are unversed in the particular areas of law covered.

Beginning researchers usually find that secondary sources in paper format are the easiest to use. In large part, this is due to the fact that their principal finding tool, the keyword subject index, is tailor-made to the medium of paper. The user of a paper index is quite likely to find additional relevant keywords, and it is easy to flip pages, following cross-references from one term to another. Paper resources also promote the serendipitous discovery of information one had no idea even existed. Even those accustomed to reading materials in electronic formats usually find that a keyword index seems less accessible when its contents are viewed scrolling down a computer screen. Given the greater efficacy of the keyword index in paper formats, a researcher using a secondary source in paper can usually find the information he or she seeks in as short of an amount of time or even shorter than if an electronic source had been employed.

What the researcher ultimately finds in a secondary source of any format is a discussion that will educate him or her about the law and the law's terms of art. Notably, it will include citations to cases, statutes, and other primary legal authorities the researcher is seeking. With minimal expenditure of time and money, the researcher using a secondary source is given a step in the door of the legal problem being investigated and has the added assurance that the citations provided are of guaranteed relevance.

Armed with these citations — and even one relevant citation is usually enough — the researcher can turn justifiably to the fee-based electronic sources. Pulling up a known citation to a relevant legal authority on these sources is much cheaper than performing a subject search to find that authority in the first place. Moreover, the authority that is pulled up by citation will have a variety of links to other relevant legal authorities, which can also be accessed at lesser cost. These additional authorities, in turn, provide links to other relevant authorities – and so it goes. Very quickly, the universe of authority related to the issue can be accessed with the least cost.

To sum up, this strategy operates on the premise that legal research can be performed most efficiently and cost-effectively if secondary sources, particularly in paper, are employed as the researcher's initial access points. With citations of known relevance in hand, the researcher then turns to the fee-based electronic databases, using them as known law suppliers rather than as initial law finders.

I. The Steps of Strategic Legal Research

There are ten basic steps of strategic legal research, each of which will be discussed in greater detail in Chapter 4:

- **Step 1:** Get the facts of the case through an effective assignment interview.

- **Step 2:** Analyze the problem, generate a list of keywords, and identify the issues to research.

- **Step 3:** Determine the governing jurisdiction.

- **Step 4:** Choose the most useful research format for the job at hand.

- **Step 5:** Begin to research in no-fee secondary sources and digests and annotated codes, all of which educate you about the law, provide citations to relevant legal authorities, and do much of the research for you.

- **Step 6:** Use fee-based legal databases to retrieve authorities by citation and employ citators to verify they remain good law.

- **Step 7:** Follow the links found in authorities retrieved in fee-based legal databases to locate additional sources, effectively employing those databases more as suppliers of known authority than as initial law finders.

- **Step 8:** If research must be initiated in fee-based legal databases through keyword subject searches, perform those searches carefully and wisely.

- **Step 9:** Alert the supervising attorney to unforeseen, major developments that are discovered in the course of research.

- **Step 10:** Stop researching when the results and the circumstances warrant.

Chapter 4
The Steps of Strategic Legal Research

Step 1: Get the facts of the case through an effective assignment interview.

It is rare for beginning junior associates to be introduced to a client's legal matter through an actual client interview. More often, a senior attorney will brief the junior associate on the client's case and request some action to be taken. The interview with the assigning attorney is critical to the successful completion of any research project.

A. Prior to the Assignment Interview

Return the assigning attorney's call immediately if you were not available to take it. Pull yourself together – physically and mentally. Appearing calm, collected, and enthusiastic makes the best impression. Be sure to bring materials for note-taking. There will be too much information to keep in your head.

B. At the Assignment Interview

The assigning attorney will relate the facts of the case and explain the problem that requires resolution on your part. Listen attentively to what the attorney says.

You have an active role to play beyond listening. Question the attorney if anything said is unclear. Think of yourself as a reporter who needs to understand the "who-what-why-when-where" of the case. Ask for this information if the attorney omits it. Should the attorney refer to an acronym, be sure you know exactly what it stands for. If you don't know, or even if you have the slightest doubt, ask what it means.

Do not leave the interview without learning the client/matter number. The client/matter number is a number assigned by the firm that uniquely identifies each matter of legal representation undertaken by the firm for each client. It is used chiefly for billing purposes. On timesheets, attorneys generally assign the client/matter number to the blocks of time they have spent working on the case. The number may also be necessary for access to photocopying and other billable services.

Verify what is expected of you. Before the interview ends, you should know the scope of the issue that requires research. Be certain you understand the nature of the work product you are expected to produce. For example, does the attorney expect a written memo or simply an oral report?

Finally, ascertain the time frame in which the work is to be completed. If an assignment from another attorney will conflict, tell the assigning attorney about it up front. Usually the two attorneys will talk to work the conflict out.

C. After the Assignment Interview

When the interview is over, go back to your desk and read over your notes. Fill in information you did not have a chance to write down. Be sure your notes are legible and written so that they can be deciphered at a later date. It is not uncommon for researchers to refer to their notes as the research process proceeds. Nor is it uncommon for researchers to be assigned follow-up research days or even months after the assignment interview. When this occurs, you will be expected to remember the facts of the case that were imparted to you initially. Thus, it is critical to create and maintain thorough notes.

Step 2: Analyze the problem, generate a list of keywords, and identify the issues to research.

Understanding the question is vital for effective legal research. Your challenge as a researcher is to find the answers to your legal questions in targeted research sources that provide the greatest value in terms of content, efficiency, and cost. If you don't understand (or worse, have not formulated) a question to research, it will be nearly impossible to evaluate the available resources to choose those best suited to your needs.

Legal research in any media, whether paper or electronic, is keyword driven. The most effective researchers bear this in mind from beginning to end.

There are two different categories of keywords: generic descriptors and terms of art. Generic descriptors are the keywords, which generally describe various aspects of the case. Researchers generate these generic descriptors through analysis of the facts of the case and use them in their initial keyword searches to locate information pertinent to their issues.

A second category of keywords is known as "terms of art." These are particular words that regularly appear in the discussion of specific legal issues. Terms of art often are not intuitive. Thus, researchers rely on general keywords to initiate their searches for relevant materials. However, once relevant materials have been found, skilled researchers examine them closely for recurring words or phrases that can be classified as terms of art. In subsequent research, particularly in electronic media, researchers will then frame their keyword searches using these terms of art.

The keyword research of beginners frequently suffers as a result of a variety of misconceptions:

- Beginning researchers often mistakenly assume that research in paper materials is old-hat. To the contrary, paper research is alive and well in the legal research arena. No one should think it is "not cool" to be seen flipping a page as opposed to typing on a keyboard. However counterintuitive it may appear in this digital age, paper sources and the indexes to them often lead researchers more quickly to the materials they need. As a general rule of thumb, the less one knows about the area of law being researched, the greater the likelihood that keyword searching will be more efficient and cost-effective if begun initially in paper resources.

- Researchers frequently think an electronic source is preferable because general keywords can be input to discover both the terms of art and relevant materials in one fell swoop. The fallacy of this argument lies in the fact that the results of electronic research are dependent entirely on the words that are input. To be blunt, lousy keywords lead to garbage. Even if one stumbles eventually on useful terms that produce useful results, a lot of time and money will have been wasted on trial and error.

- Inexperienced researchers sometimes think that trial and error can be justified when the electronic resource involves no access charges (i.e., it is free to use.) They forget that time is money, at least in law firms. Attorneys in firms must account for every six minutes they spend on a client matter, including all time engaged in fruitless searches. Time wasted is money that either must be billed to the client or written off. Even in a non-profit legal environment, time wasted is

time that could have been spent doing something else –
maybe even going home at a decent hour.

- Although electronic keyword searching makes more
sense if the researcher knows the terms of art
applicable to the issue, he or she should not assume
that the search functions of electronic resources are
purely intuitive. To be sure, the basic search functions
of these resources are just that – basic. However, most
electronic resources also have advanced search
functions, which can make search results more focused
and on-point. Some advanced search functions even
compensate, to a degree, for a researcher's lack of
knowledge of applicable keywords. Take the trouble to
find and read the advanced search instructions.
Advanced searches usually do not cost any more than
basic searches, so why not use the electronic resources
at hand to their fullest capacity.

A. Begin by Evaluating the Problem Through Keywords

Since most legal research requires the use of keywords to
access relevant information, it makes sense and is most efficient
to analyze your case from the get-go in those terms. The goal is
to generate a list of keywords that helps formulate or solidify
the issue to be researched in your mind and that includes the
categories of keywords, which are the foundation of the
prevailing systems for the retrieval of legal information.

Think about the facts of the case in terms of the:

- Kinds of people involved;

- Kinds of places involved;

- Kinds of things involved;

- Kinds of actions involved;

- Kinds of law involved;

- Kinds of defenses that could be pled; and

- Kinds of relief that could be sought.

Prepare a written list broken down by these categories. Under each category, write down words and their synonyms, which describe the facts of the case in relation to that category. Your words should start specifically and become progressively more general so that you also have words, which conceptualize in broader terms the situation involved.

After generating a string of words for each category, review the list as a whole. Consider the relationships between the categories and the words you have listed. Frame and write down a question that encompasses words from each of the categories. It is very important that you actually write this question down because the act of writing helps concentrate your thinking and solidifies the issue in your mind.

B. An Illustration of Keyword Fact Analysis

The problem below typifies the kind of research assignment that a junior associate might be asked to undertake. The associate must determine whether the client, a hotel, is liable for an injury sustained at the hotel by one of its guests.

First, the researcher assembles the complete facts of the case:

Clutch City Lodge owns a boutique hotel in Houston, Texas. Abraham Abbott, a guest from New York, suffered a minor head injury when a bathroom medicine cabinet fell off the wall and struck him. An investigation subsequent to the accident revealed that the screws attaching the cabinet to the wall had worked loose. A housekeeper had cleaned the cabinet one hour before the incident occurred and noticed nothing amiss. All of the medicine cabinets in the Lodge's 40 rooms are identical and there had been no prior indications that any had become unstable. The Lodge would like to know whether it is liable for Abbott's injury.

Second, the researcher categorizes the facts in terms of their relation to the legal problem and lists both specific and general keywords that could describe each fact within each category:

PEOPLE:

- Abraham Abbott, guest, visitor
- housekeeper, inspector

PLACES:

- Houston, Texas
- hotel, motel, lodging, guest room, bathroom

THINGS:

- medicine cabinet (found in all rooms), fixture, property defect

ACTIVITIES:

- injury, pain, and suffering
- falling cabinet, accident
- prior cleaning of cabinet, no reports of defects

LAW:

- tort, premises liability, product liability

POTENTIAL DEFENSES:

- Proprietor's lack of knowledge of defect
- guest's assumption of risk
- guest's contributory negligence

POTENTIAL REMEDIES:

- compensation for medical treatment, injury, pain, and suffering

Finally, the researcher reviews the list as a whole to spot potentially important relationships in the fact pattern. Here, for example, it could be significant that the cabinet had passed inspection immediately before the accident and that no prior defect had been reported in it or any of the identical cabinets in the Lodge. The researcher drafts a research question that incorporates these relationships, using the most likely keywords from each of the list's categories:

Under Texas law, is a hotel liable in tort or products liability for an accident to a guest who was injured as a result of a defective fixture in his hotel room, if the defect was not discovered during a prior inspection of the room by hotel personnel and no reports had occurred previously of defects in the identical fixtures in the hotel's other rooms?

C. The End Result of Keyword Fact Analysis

You now have a ready-made list of keywords that pertain to the categories according to which the finding tools of paper and electronic legal research resources are organized. The words on the list are the words you will use in these resources to find the information you need. Don't worry about whether your words precisely hit the nail on the head. At the very least, they probably will be sufficient to lead to links to other words that relate to your issue more precisely. You can and should revise your list as you learn more about the law involved. Indeed, as you discover that certain words or phrases are terms of art pertaining to the issue, substitute these terms in subsequent searches.

In addition, by framing the issue in terms of the principal facts of the case, you have created a question that serves two-fold: It will refresh your recollection of the situation if there is an interval between the assignment and the beginning of your actual research, and it also provides a suitable basis for evaluating the kinds of research tools that will be best suited to your needs and skills.

Step 3: Determine the governing jurisdiction.

It is critical at the outset to ascertain the jurisdiction whose law will apply to the issue at hand. The jurisdiction determines what law is binding primary authority and what law is merely persuasive. If binding authority sufficiently answers the question, there may be no reason to look further.

Knowing the jurisdiction narrows the scope of the search, saving you time and the client money. Although electronic research sources make searching across jurisdictions relatively easy, the result could be a large pool of hits. Many will be, at best, merely persuasive or, at worst, irrelevant. Sorting through all of them could be time consuming. The danger also arises that materials you really do need could be buried in the unmanageable pool of hits.

A. How to Determine the Jurisdiction

It is certainly appropriate to question the assigning attorney about the applicable jurisdiction during the assignment interview. If that is not possible, check to see if any pleadings already have been filed in the matter. They will indicate the jurisdiction. Also, if the matter involves a contractual dispute, the contract itself may include a choice of law clause that stipulates the jurisdiction in which subsequent disputes are to be litigated.

It could be that the jurisdiction is the very first issue you will need to research. Look closely at the facts. Does the problem seem to involve a federal interest as opposed to a more localized state one? If it seems more like a state issue, check in which states the parties resided and where the events occurred. Of course, you never want to base your research on a mere hunch, but these questions will help you to prioritize the kinds of research sources in which to begin.

One option is to consult treatises (a fancy word for reference books) that relate to the kind of law involved. If you have access to a catalogued law library, begin with a keyword search in its catalogue. Titles can also be identified through a Google search. Input "[Subject] law research guide." For example, if your issue related to airplanes, you might Google "Aviation Research Guide." This kind of search often leads to practice guides prepared by academic law librarians.

When multiple jurisdictions appear to be involved, consult treatises on federal or state procedure. Some of the standbys are the following:

- Federal Procedure, Lawyers Edition, 1981-date. Also available on Westlaw.

- Moore's Federal Practice, 3d ed., 1997-date. Also available on Lexis.

- Wright & Miller, Federal Practice and Procedure, 3d ed., 1998- date. Also available on Westlaw.

- Texas Civil Procedure: Trial & Appellate Practice, 2008-date. Also available on Lexis.

Step 4: Choose the most useful research format for the job at hand.

Now that you have a question to research and know the jurisdiction in which to seek the answer to that question, it is time to choose the best sources for your research. Think of legal research as like a battle. No general goes into battle without a plan, and you shouldn't embark on legal research without a plan either. Remember the goal: to do the job well in a time- and cost-effective manner.

Choosing the format of the materials in which to research is an important decision when multiple options are available to you. In some instances, the same source will be available in different formats. In other instances, a relevant source may be available in one format, e.g., paper, while another equally good source is available electronically. Choose research formats that are best suited to your knowledge and skill level. For example, paper materials are among the most user-friendly, particularly for beginning researchers and those unfamiliar with the area of the law to which the issue pertains. Try to educate yourself about the available research materials before you have to research. In your down time, familiarize yourself with those that are used most commonly in your practice area.

This section explains the common formats you will encounter, discusses their pros and cons, and offers general tips for using them successfully.

A. Paper Research Sources

Paper is the traditional format for legal research sources and, notwithstanding the plethora of electronic alternatives, remains a viable format, at least for the near future. Paper resources may appear as a single volume or comprise multi-volume sets. Most feature comprehensive keyword indexes and tables of contents. Paper materials are usually updated by supplements, pocket parts, or loose-leaf substitutions or insertions.

1. Advantages

The great advantage of a paper source is that, once it has been purchased, users incur no subsequent access costs. Paper materials also offer a significant advantage to novice legal researchers or researchers who are unfamiliar with a particular area of the law. The indexes of paper materials are usually still prepared by humans with the intent of guiding the uninitiated to desired content. The ability to browse adjacent sections also encourages the serendipitous discovery of useful information, which may be lacking in electronic sources that carry the reader to an isolated body of material. Moreover, since paper materials have usually been vetted by the experienced law librarians or practitioners who purchased them, researchers have some assurance that the information within is authoritative and accurate.

2. Disadvantages

The greatest disadvantages of paper materials are that relevant sections must be photocopied manually and the volumes will probably not be accessible off-site. They also cannot be updated as quickly as electronic sources. Researchers extremely familiar with the law and its terms of art may find research in paper to be slower than electronic research (but the reverse is generally true when researchers lack knowledge of the field.)

3. User Tips

a. Indexes

Indexes are alphabetical listings of keywords with location references to related content in the text. Sometimes these references include abbreviations. If that is the case, there should be a key explaining their meaning at the beginning of the index or in the introductory materials of the text.

Index entries are usually broken down into subcategories, which are arranged alphabetically by sub-keywords. Patience is a virtue when using indexes. Scan down the complete list of subcategories. You may discover additional relevant keywords. You may also see keywords that trigger new insights about the problem. Be sure to keeps notes of the keywords you looked at and employ any newly-discovered keywords in subsequent searches.

Indexes commonly employ a variety of references from one keyword to another. The most common are the following:

- *See* (check another keyword instead).

- *See also* (check another keyword in addition to this one).

- *See herein* (check instead another sub-category of the keyword you are currently consulting).

b. Tables of Contents

A table of contents is a roadmap of the text that lists the titles (in the order in which they appear) of chapters, subchapters, sections, sub-sections, etc. A table of contents of the entire text usually appears at the beginning of the first volume and sometimes appears at the beginning of each volume of multi-volume works. Sometimes an auxiliary table of contents can be found at the beginning of each chapter, listing the section titles within that chapter in sequential order.

Scanning through a table of contents may offer insights about the issue you had not thought of. It is also a good idea to scan the table of contents when a keyword search in the index proves unfruitful.

c. Spine Labels

Legal encyclopedias and other multi-volume works, which cover independent topics in alphabetical order, often have labels on their spines on which are printed keywords identifying the range of topics included in each volume. For example: "Cat – Contracts" would signify that the volume includes those categories as well as any other categories falling alphabetically between them, e.g., "Colleges and Universities."

Suppose your research involves contracts and you see "Contracts" listed on the spine of a legal encyclopedia. The temptation is great to dive right in. However, ultimately, this could prove an unwise choice. Although, under the circumstances, first performing a keyword search in the general index might seem superfluous, the search is usually time well spent. Whenever you neglect to search the index, you risk missing relevant material that is covered under a different topic. You also miss out on the educational function of indexes as guides to additional keywords and as sources of illumination concerning unconsidered aspects of your research problem.

B. In-House Electronic Resources

The term "in-house electronic resources" refers to electronic legal reference sources that the employer has purchased by subscription. Many are electronic versions of sources that either also appear in paper or else once did. They are accessed primarily through keyword searches. Their degree of technical sophistication varies widely.

1. Advantages

Like paper materials, in-house electronic resources bear no user access costs and carry the added assurance that some knowledgeable person deemed them to be sufficiently authoritative to warrant their purchase. However, unlike printed materials, they are accessible from the desktop, may be accessible off-site, and the materials within can usually be copied or downloaded. In addition, they may be (but are not always) updated more frequently.

2. Disadvantages

The electronic search functions in these materials often do not provide the kinds of guidance in the form of *see* references and the like that paper indexes provide to guide researchers who lack a firm knowledge of the law to relevant material. Browsing is also less easy than in paper. In addition, graphs, charts, and illustrations appearing in the paper versions may not be reproduced in these electronic formats. Also, if the resource is transmitted electronically from the provider, it will become unavailable if the subscription is not renewed.

Sometimes an electronic source is little more than a PDF file of its paper version. Thankfully, this phenomenon is becoming increasingly rare in commercially produced sources, but it still occurs in some materials produced under government sponsorship. Using resources with this defect can be an exercise in frustration. Methodologies that work efficiently in paper formats do not always translate well to electronic media, particularly if the electronic materials load very slowly, which often occurs. When one encounters resources of this kind and their paper counterparts are available, the paper resources are probably the more efficient bet.

3. User Tips

a. Read the Directions

Admittedly, it is hard to resist the urge when using these electronic resources to rush in, throwing words into the basic search function the same way most of us employ Google. However, little standardization exists among products and many are not as intuitive to use as one might think. Force yourself to link to and read the explanation of the search features and how they work. Think of the time spent learning their use as an investment that leads to better results and time-saving in the long run.

b. Use Advanced Search Functions

If the source has an advanced search option (and most now do), it should be used in preference to the basic search function. Advanced searching allows for a more tailored search with more targeted results so that you do not have to wade through masses of irrelevant hits. Common features of advanced search functions include:

- The thesaurus function, which suggests alternative keywords based on the words you have input;

- The capability to capture variants of keyword variants, e.g. "woman" and "women;"

- The capability to stipulate the presence of certain words and the exclusion of others in the search results;

- Features that capture exact phrases, e.g., "products liability;" and

- Features that limit the results by date, type of material or source, court, and judges or attorneys involved.

C. Lexis and Westlaw

Lexis and Westlaw maintain their status as the preeminent, commercial, fee-based providers of electronic legal information. Both offer a comprehensive range of primary sources covering all U.S. jurisdictions (and some foreign) with editorial enhancements to make finding related materials very easy. Each also provides access to equivalent (although not identical) secondary sources and to nonlegal materials such as newspapers and transcripts of news-related television and radio broadcasts.

Materials can be retrieved in several ways: by keyword searching, by known citation, by following links to other sources cited in the source itself, and by utilizing editorial digesting features, which link a source to other sources dealing with the same issue or point of law. Both services also maintain readily accessible citators that alert the researcher to the current status of primary authorities as good law and provide lists of other sources that have cited them.

Both Lexis and Westlaw are currently in a state of flux in regard to the format of their search platforms. Each has initiated a new platform that incorporates features that approximate a Google-search experience. Lexis' new platform is Lexis Advance and Westlaw's is WestlawNext. At the present, these new platforms coexist with the providers' original search platforms, Lexis.com and Westlaw Classic. Although Lexis and Westlaw have announced plans to abandon their old platforms sometime in the future, some legal employers continue to retain the older versions.

The fee structures of Lexis and Westlaw are very complicated and unique to each. Both allow firms and other legal employers to tailor plans to their needs in respect to the kinds of materials that can be accessed. Many employers negotiate to receive access at a fixed monthly or yearly rate. Even so, no researcher should assume that the negotiation of a fixed rate gives him or her license to use Lexis or Westlaw with abandon. A fixed rate does not change the fact that inefficient use of Lexis and Westlaw results in additional charges to clients for the additional attorney time expended. And, even if one does not work in a firm, efficiency is highly valued. Researchers should also keep in mind that unexpectedly high Lexis and Westlaw usage will almost certainly lead to a higher rate when the period of the fixed rate expires.

1. User Tips

a. Employ Known Authority Searches Whenever Possible

Known authority searching provides the most cost-effective (i.e., cheapest) access to Lexis and Westlaw and is the basis of the research methodology explained in this guide. Known authority searching encompasses more than simply inputting the citation to an authority one desires to see. Once that authority appears on the screen, known authority searching also occurs when the researcher follows links to other authorities cited by the initial authority. It occurs, again, when editorial links appended to the authority by Lexis or Westlaw are followed to access additional materials, which Lexis or Westlaw believes are of related interest.

b. Frame Keyword Subject Searches Thoughtfully and Carefully, Particularly When Using the Original Search Platforms of Lexis and Westlaw

Step 8 of the research methodology explains keyword subject searching in Lexis and Westlaw in detail. At this juncture, it is sufficient to note that, while careful and thoughtful searching is important in any research database, it becomes absolutely critical when performing searches in the original platforms of Lexis and Westlaw. Both platforms levy a charge for every search, the magnitude of which depends on the size and type of the database in which the search is carried out. Accordingly, off-the-cuff trial and error searching of the kind commonly practiced in Google becomes prohibitively expensive when one logs on to these platforms. (Note: although the new platforms, Lexis Advance and WestlawNext, have abandoned the per-search charge, they have instituted a charge for each result viewed, which carries its own consequences, described below.)

c. Focus Subject Searches

Because subject searches can result either directly or indirectly in the heftiest charges on Lexis and Westlaw, a researcher should craft the search with great care. The more focused it is, the better.

An intelligent subject search is focused in a number of ways. Focusing occurs in the first instance through the careful choice of search terms. The most reliable searches are those that employ the terms of art commonly used in relation to the issue. Barring knowledge of those, the researcher – before even logging in to Lexis or Westlaw -- should analyze the facts of the case to identify the general keywords that relate to the issue (see Step 2). Armed with those, the researcher should also take advantage of the thesaurus features found in the original search platforms of Lexis and Westlaw. These features suggest additional words based on the words already input. Sometimes, these additional words include the terms of art.

Focusing also occurs through limiting the jurisdiction of the search. Although neither Lexis Advance nor WestlawNext requires the researcher to choose a jurisdiction as a prerequisite for a search, restricting the jurisdiction makes a lot of sense. It saves time and money by reducing the number of results the researcher has to sort through. For example, if one's question were governed by Texas law, it is hard to see the point of a search of the laws of all 50 states. It is highly probable that a search restricted to Texas primary authorities will provide the answer. In the rare instances that it does not, one can always expand the jurisdiction. Although other states' practices might well be quite fascinating, practicing attorneys rarely have the luxury in terms of time and money to pursue matters of purely academic interest.

Both Lexis and Westlaw also permit researchers to focus still further within the results of a search at no additional cost. Even the most carefully-thought-out search sometimes results in an unwieldy number of hits or in a mix of relevant and irrelevant items owing perhaps to the unforeseen consequences of a keyword having a double meaning. These focus features allow researchers to add restrictive modifiers to create a more manageable and relevant list of results.

d. Read Before You Click, Particularly in Lexis Advance and WestlawNext

Each entry on the list of results of a search in Lexis and Westlaw includes excerpts from the authority containing the keywords of the search and, perhaps, other explanatory information that allows the user to determine whether the item is relevant or not. Clicking on the result pulls up the full text, which carries significant consequences for users of Lexis Advance and WestlawNext. Although the initial searches in these new platforms incur no costs, a fee is charged every time the researcher clicks on a search result to view it in full text. At, for example, $12 a click, indiscriminate selection soon leads to a hefty charge.

Even if a click does not result in a charge (as in the original platforms of Lexis and Westlaw), indiscriminate selection wastes precious time. An intelligent researcher scans through the excerpts of all (or at least a considerable number) of the results and, on the basis of that examination, prioritizes his or her selections. For example, if the same relevant language appeared in the opinions of a number of the cases on a list of search results, including opinions of the jurisdiction's highest court, the researcher sensibly would select those high court opinions in preference to lower court opinions. So, too, would it be more sensible to select opinions relating most closely to the fact situation of the issue before opening up those of more marginal connection. In short, the intelligent researcher, recognizing that an attorney's time is a valuable commodity, whether it is being billed to a client or not, always accords priority to sources likely to produce the greatest benefits.

e. Remember That Patience Is a Virtue

Just because a search is electronic does not mean that the answer will jump out at the researcher. Do not assume that the best results of a search always appear at the beginning of the list of hits. It is not uncommon for the "needle in the haystack" to be most useful, and that may appear far down the list. A researcher who lacks the patience to scan through all or a good portion of the results may miss the very case he or she seeks.

D. Bloomberg Law

Entering the market in 2009, Bloomberg Law has positioned itself as a major competitor to Lexis and Westlaw for subscription-based legal content. Bloomberg Law's primary authority content – state and federal statutes, court opinions, and administrative rules and regulations – compares favorably to that of Lexis and Westlaw. Its citator, BCite, also approximates Lexis' Shepards and Westlaw's Key Cite with comprehensive notations of both direct history and citing references.

At present, however, Bloomberg Law differs considerably from Lexis and Westlaw in a number of ways, some very good and others less so.

1. Advantages

Bloomberg Law's fee structure provides unlimited use for a flat rate. Thus, the researcher can perform unlimited searches *and* open and read their results without incurring additional charges.

For attorneys engaged in transactional or regulatory practice, Bloomberg Law will prove a godsend. Bloomberg Law's inclusion of Bureau of National Affairs (BNA) publications provides ready access to advisory bulletins, opinion letters, administrative law judge rulings, and a wealth of transactional and regulatory secondary source materials. Bloomberg Law's affiliation with its parent, Bloomberg L.P., a leading provider of business and financial news, also allows it to provide access to news and financial analyses of particular industries as well as of individual companies.

Bloomberg Law allows keyword searches of the federal dockets. Indeed, its docket database offers a comparable alternative to the U.S. Government's Pacer system. Bloomberg Law's docket retrieval service, however, provides a significant advantage. Although a docket retrieved for the first time incurs a fee equivalent to that charged by Pacer, that docket then becomes available free of charge for all subsequent Bloomberg Law users.

2. Disadvantages

At present, Bloomberg Law searches can be performed using only Boolean search methodology. Bloomberg Law does not offer a natural language alternative.

Bloomberg Law does not include annotated versions of state and federal codes. Although a "Court Opinions" link at the top of the statutory text functions as a substitute and allows keyword searching, it lacks the facility of use of a standard annotated code.

Aside from law reviews, Bloomberg Law lacks Lexis' and Westlaw's range of the kind of secondary source materials of greatest value to the general practitioner, such as legal encyclopedias, American Law Reports, and general treatises.

Bloomberg Law has not yet developed a comprehensive topical headnote system akin to Lexis' headnotes and Westlaw's topics and key numbers. Accordingly, on Bloomberg Law, the linkages from one case to related cases are largely restricted to the cases cited within a case and to the references found using BCite.

E. Internet Research Sources

The internet is the first source to which many lawyers turn. There is nothing wrong with that if — and it's a big if — legal researchers use the internet as intelligently as other reference sources. Too many practitioners, seduced by the internet's ready availability and the seemingly "free lunch" it provides, lose sight of efficiency and cost-effectiveness as soon as Google appears on their screens. It is also important to remember that Google is not the only game in town. In addition to Bing and Yahoo, there are many specialized search engines worthy of attorneys' consideration.

1. Advantages

It's free, it's there, and it provides access to extremely useful information, much of which was formerly difficult and costly to obtain. Nor can it be overlooked that the internet is fertile ground for attorneys engaged in pre-trial discovery.

2. Disadvantages

The internet is not really as free as it seems. Time becomes no less valuable when it is spent on the internet. Internet research that takes longer than the equivalent research would have taken in another free source wastes attorneys' time and needlessly expends clients' money. In weighing the relative benefits of the internet versus other sources, attorneys should bear in mind that information placed on the internet is not vetted for authoritativeness like the information appearing in secondary sources produced by publishers whose reputations are on the line. Thus, while an attorney still must verify the accuracy of information obtained from any secondary source, vetting information derived from the internet may require additional effort on the attorney's part. In addition to that, the internet does not encompass the value-added features found in other information providers, tools such as indexes with *see* references that direct the uninformed to the information they need. Thus, the internet is often less efficient and cost-effective than it may initially seem.

3. User Tips

a. Keywords Still Matter

Mindless and uninformed searches on the internet are as big of a time-waster as anywhere else.

b. Check for the Expiration Date

A staggering amount of out-of-date information appears on the internet. Any internet source worth its salt should include a date indicating when it was last updated. A source that does not should immediately be deemed suspect and treated with great caution.

c. All Search Engines Are Not Alike

Every search engine has a unique algorithm that governs its searches. Thus, the same search performed on different search engines usually produces somewhat different results.

Individual search engines compile their own searchable databases, using "spiders" that crawl through the web, link by link, indexing the words on each page. Google, Bing and Yahoo are prime examples. Most individual search engines have, in addition to their basic search function, an advanced search function. These advanced search functions allow users to better tailor their searches by specifying words, word phrases, and word combinations that should be included in the search and by excluding those that should not. Advance search functions also commonly allow users to restrict results by language and date. Particularly useful are commands that direct the search engine to identify other sites that have linked a specified site or commands that identify sites similar to a specified cite.

Meta search engines do not compile their own databases; rather, they search multiple sets of existing databases. Dogpile and Yippy are examples. Although meta search engines provide a snapshot of what is available on the web, they are only as good as the databases they search, and not all search Google. Meta search engines also may not have advanced search functions.

d. Don't Ignore the Invisible Web

The invisible web refers to online materials that are not accessible through search engines. These materials can be very scholarly and include library catalogues and periodical or statistical databases. Some, however, require user passwords, which place them beyond the reach of the general user.

To locate materials on the invisible web, perform a general web search using the phrase "[subject] database." For example, to locate materials relating to animal law, one might go to Google and input "animal law database."

Links to the invisible web can also be found using directories of databases. Useful directories include:

- ipl2, a directory of databases compiled by librarians;

- Infomine, a directory of academic and scholarly resources; and

- Guide to Law Online (a directory created by the Law Library of Congress).

The web pages of academic law libraries and the web sites of scholarly organizations also frequently include links to useful databases on the invisible web.

Step 5: Begin to research in no-fee secondary sources and digests and annotated codes, all of which educate you about the law, provide citations to relevant legal authorities, and do much of the research for you.

Always begin to research in materials that promise to do as much of the research legwork as possible. The goal is to find ready-made lists of relevant primary authorities and links to additional authorities. Skilled researchers routinely utilize the research of others. Indeed, in the cost- and time-conscious climate in which attorneys operate, it would be foolish to reinvent the wheel. Time is better spent evaluating the relevance, currency, and accuracy of materials found by others and augmenting them with authorities of more recent vintage. All of these reasons explain why strategic researchers begin their work in secondary sources and digests and annotated codes.

A secondary source is a work that explains the law but is not the law itself. Secondary sources include such materials as legal encyclopedias, treatises, and periodicals. Researchers use secondary sources to get a handle on an unfamiliar legal topic. They provide an overview of the law and introduce the terms of art, or language commonly applied, in reference to it. Equally important, secondary sources include citations to governing primary authority.

Whatever one's degree of expertise in the law, secondary sources are useful for a number of reasons. First, they provide an overview of the law that ties its components together in a neat package. Second, they introduce the researcher to the law's terms of art, the knowledge of which is helpful for research in other sources. Third, they provide the researcher a degree of assurance that he or she has not overlooked anything of critical importance to the law's application. Finally, secondary sources include citations to primary authority and, in so doing, give the researcher a significant leg-up in the research process. Thus, most researchers profit from the overview of the law that a secondary source provides. In fact, secondary sources promote efficiency by allowing attorneys to get up to speed in the law more quickly than if they tried to piece it together themselves from the primary source materials. And, secondary sources in paper, because of the prevalence of *see* cites in their subject indexes that guide the user from one keyword to a better keyword, provide still greater assurance that even the most novice researcher will be able to find the materials he or she needs rapidly.

Digests and annotated codes include quasi-secondary editorial content created by commercial legal publishers, which links related primary authorities to each other. Examples of quasi-secondary editorial content are the headnotes based on the West Publishing Company's Topic and Key Number System, which serve as the foundation of digests, and the annotations in annotated codes, all of which will be discussed more fully below. These editorial materials are "quasi-secondary" in the sense that they, like standard secondary sources, have been created to place primary authorities in context and illuminate the relationships between them. An advantage of the quasi-secondary content is that it frequently appears in conjunction with the primary authority to which it refers. However, it must be understood that this content is not itself primary authority and should never be quoted or cited as such.

Researchers should not reject paper secondary sources from the mistaken belief that the electronic keyword subject search often is necessarily the ultimate time-saver. Indeed, the vision of primary materials falling directly into one's lap seconds after a single electronic search possesses an incredible allure. However, for most researchers, that vision is more a dream than reality. Although all legal research media are keyword driven, electronic media is particularly unforgiving if researchers are unfamiliar with the terms of art commonly used in connection with the law they are researching. Researchers lacking such knowledge are likely to waste a lot of time inputting unfruitful search terms or engaging in overly general searches that result in too many hits to process effectively and efficiently. Even worse, because of their lack of understanding, these researchers may not even recognize relevant law when they find it; alternatively, they may spend hours following rabbit trails in pursuit of the irrelevant. Finally, if a researcher's unfamiliarity with the law results in an electronic search being framed too narrowly, he or she runs the risk of not becoming aware in a timely manner of potential exceptions or defenses to the law or alternative legal theories.

An important adjunct to secondary sources and digests and annotated codes is the keyword subject index. The keyword subject index is conceived to allow researchers who know very little, or even nothing at all, about the law they seek to access materials relevant to their needs. The keyword entries in the index correlate to the kinds of people, places, things, causes of actions, and avenues of relief to which the materials they reference relate. Recall that these categories are precisely the categories used previously to analyze the facts of a case and to develop the issue to research. Thus, it is not fatal if the general keywords derived from that analysis do not precisely match the terms of art used in the primary authorities themselves (say, for example, the analysis resulted in the word "motels" but the statute is framed using the word "inns"). At least one of the general keywords is likely to appear in the index with guidance to help the researcher on his or her way. For example, "motels" might appear in the index with a reference to "*see* inns and innkeepers"; in turn, "inns and innkeepers" might be followed by a reference to the section in the code that discusses the law related to places of lodging.

Using the keyword subject indexes to no-fee secondary sources and digests and annotated codes, the researcher can quickly find citations to primary authorities of demonstrated relevance. As explained in successive sections, a single citation provides access to other legal authorities relating to the topic and also allows the quick retrieval of these authorities using the most cost-effective applications of fee-based electronic databases.

This first part of this section describes secondary sources, digests, annotated codes, and their various components. A methodology for using these materials is explained in the second part.

A. Useful Secondary Sources

1. National Legal Encyclopedias

Legal encyclopedias provide a wide-ranging overview of the law of a jurisdiction with the greatest emphasis on its common law. They are available in Lexis and Westlaw and in other electronic formats. In paper form, they appear as large multi-volume sets. Entries are arranged by topics in alphabetical order. They tend to focus more on generalities than on fact-specifics, and on well-established principles than on cutting-edge developments. The degree of citation to primary authorities varies among encyclopedias. Updating occurs through pocket parts, which are slotted at the end of each volume. The general keyword indexes to legal encyclopedias typically appear as several volumes at the end of the sets. They are printed in paperback and updated annually.

There are two major legal encyclopedias, which are national in scope: *Corpus Juris Secundum* and *American Jurisprudence*.

a. *Corpus Juris Secundum*

Corpus Juris Secundum takes a microcosmic approach to the law, its discussions being heavily footnoted with citations to numerous cases from multiple jurisdictions. Discussions are cross-referenced to the applicable West topic and key numbers (see the discussion of these below), promoting ready access in West digests to additional citations to primary authorities.

b. *American Jurisprudence*

American Jurisprudence takes a more macrocosmic approach to the law. It cites fewer cases in its discussions, preferring to focus on those it deems to be most illustrative or of landmark status. A unique feature is its citation to applicable annotations in *American Law Reports* and to related sections in the restatements of the law (both of which are discussed below).

2. State Legal Encyclopedias

Legal encyclopedias treating the laws of an individual state are available for select jurisdictions. Examples include *Texas Jurisprudence* and *New York Jurisprudence*. Their formats and manners of updating mirror those of the national encyclopedias.

3. *American Law Reports* (ALRs)

American Law Reports, which encompasses hundreds of volumes in its paper format, is a legal researcher's godsend. Several different series of multi-volume sets have been issued from 1919 to the present. The earliest series encompassed annotations dealing with both federal and state issues. Beginning in 1969, federal and state issues have been covered separately in series designated respectively as "ALR Feds" and "ALRs."

Although *American Law Reports* reprints decisions of significant cases, hardly anyone uses it as a source of primary authority.   Rather, researchers use its annotations. Each annotation is essentially an essay that addresses a fact-specific issue of either statutory or common law. In this respect, the annotations fill the void left by the legal encyclopedias' concentration on generalities. Annotations tend also to focus more on cutting-edge areas of the law than do encyclopedias.

An ALR annotation is generally a non-scholarly discussion, written by a legal professional, on a specific legal issue as it relates to a particular fact situation, e.g., a tenant's rights when a landlord fails to make repairs. The author focuses more on the description of cases with assorted fact variations and outcomes than on legal analysis. Each annotation includes the following:

- A table of contents;

- A topical keyword index;

- A list of related sources, including citations to *American Jurisprudence*, West topic and key numbers, and suggested keyword searches;

- A table of jurisdictions indicating the sections of the annotation where cases from a particular jurisdiction are discussed; and

- The discussion itself, which progresses from the general to the more specific aspects of the issue.

Annotations are updated through pocket parts appended to the volumes in which the annotations appear. Older annotations are eventually superseded by new ones and, indeed, most of the annotations in the earlier series of the ALR have now been superseded. Users should check the Annotation History Table, arranged by ALR citation, at the end of the General Index to determine whether any given annotation has been replaced by a more current one.

Indexes and the ALR Digest help the researcher locate relevant ALR annotations.

Indexes to the ALR are of several kinds. The General Index to the 2nd and all later series, federal and state, is the preferred index. It provides keyword subject access to all of the annotations in these series with *see* references to help readers locate materials of interest. The ALR Quick Index, on the other hand, is an abridged version of the General Index. Because it is not nearly so comprehensive in scope as the General Index, the Quick Index should be used only if the General Index is not available. Lastly, the General Index to the 1st series covers the years 1919-1948. However, researchers rarely use this index because most of the annotations from this period have been superseded.

The ALR Digest arranges all un-superseded ALR annotations from all of the ALR series in accordance with the West topic and key number system (explained below.) It does the same with the cases reported in the ALR volumes. Users ascertain the pertinent topic and key numbers through keyword searching in the Descriptive Word Index at the end of the Digest.

4. Legal Periodicals

Legal periodicals take a variety of forms: law reviews, bar journals, and independent publications.

a. Law Reviews

Law reviews are generally published by and affiliated with law schools. They feature articles written by law professors and other legal professionals and also include "notes" or "comments," which are shorter pieces written by second- or third-year law students. Law review articles provide an in-depth, scholarly treatment of legal issues with copious footnotes to primary and secondary sources. They are a particularly good source for discussions of cutting-edge legal issues, which may not have been treated elsewhere.

b. Bar Journals

Bar journals are periodicals published by and affiliated with national, state, or local bar associations. They tend to focus on non-scholarly treatments of developments and issues currently affecting the practice of law. Issues of substantive law, if presented at all, are usually not covered in great depth.

c. Independent Journals

Independent journals may be published by commercial publishers, professional organizations, or scholarly associations. Their focus and treatment of legal issues varies, ranging from the substantive to the practice-related and from scholarly to more general-reader orientations.

Perhaps more than any other facet of legal research, technology has revolutionized the way articles in legal periodicals are located and accessed. The cumbersome, cumulative paper indexes that only provided citations have been superseded by electronic services which, through keyword searching, provide not only citations to but also, in some circumstances, the full texts of articles in law reviews and other legal periodicals. The key electronic finding tools include:

- **Multi-resource Electronic Portals** A multi-resource electronic portal is a single search engine that allows a user, through a single keyword search, to access all electronic periodical databases to which a firm or law library subscribes, often with full-text capability. The portal is tailored to the specific resources and needs of the firm or library. Thus, the content of portals varies widely. They may encompass both legal and nonlegal databases. Because the materials to which the portals provide access have already been purchased up-front through subscription, users generally incur no access costs for their searches. Most portals allow users to specify whether they wish to search all or specified databases within the portal. Portals generally feature advanced search functions. Some include the capability to limit search results by date, jurisdiction, etc.

- **Hein-On-Line** Available separately or bundled into a portal, Hein-On-Line provides access to legal and multi-disciplinary journals with full-text capability. It includes materials published prior to 1980.

- **Legal Trac** Legal Trac is a keyword finding tool to articles in legal journals and legal newspapers that were published from 1980 forward. Some articles are available full-text.

- **Index to Legal Periodicals** Full Text Index to Legal Periodicals Full Text provides keyword access to articles and book reviews in legal journals with full-text capability. Coverage begins with 1995.

- **Lexis and Westlaw** Both services feature extensive periodical databases, subject to user access costs. Although Lexis and Westlaw provide access to most law reviews, the dates of their coverage are not identical. The availability of other types of legal periodicals varies more widely, with Lexis including some not on Westlaw and vice versa. Lexis and Westlaw also have related databases covering newspapers and transcripts of radio and television programs. Articles cited in Lexis' and Westlaw's citators (Shepard's and KeyCite, respectively) and in case opinions can usually be retrieved directly by clicking on their citations.

5. Treatises

Treatises are works that treat a particular area or aspect of the law. They appear in a variety of formats, including paper, CD-ROM, and online. The authority of treatises varies and not all are equally respected or trustworthy. Some deal with an entire field, while others concentrate on discrete issues within fields. Paper formats usually include keyword general indexes.

Updating of treatises may occur through the publication of entirely new editions or by augmenting existing editions through supplemental volumes, pocket-parts, loose-leaf inserts, online revisions, etc. The user should never assume that a treatise in any format is up-to-date. It is not unusual for law libraries to keep treatises on their shelves that are no longer updated. The same may be true of treatises on CD-ROM. However, libraries generally post a notice indicating that updating has been discontinued.

Treatises may be located in several ways: Performing a keyword search in the library catalogue of your firm or law school library is one of the easiest ways to identify relevant treatises. Most library catalogues provide references to treatises held by the library in all media, not just paper. If a treatise is found in paper, remember that materials relating to the same subject are generally shelved together. Be sure to scan near-by volumes for additional sources of information.

References to treatises can also be sought online. Simply Input "[subject] practice guide" in Google or some other general search engine. One useful online guide to legal treatises is Treatises by Subject, prepared by the Heafy Law Library of Santa Clara Law School, found at http://lawguides.scu.edu/treatises.

Finally, advice about appropriate treatises can be sought from a law librarian or a senior attorney who practices in the field.

6. Restatements

Restatements are the product of the American Law Institute, which was organized in 1923. The Institute seeks to create a uniform, national American common law through the redrafting and publication of common law principles in a single rule-like source. Written in a deliberative process by committees of experts, the Restatements are scholarly and authoritative. Each common law principle appears first as a rule, which is then followed by commentary explaining it. Although these rules, as drafted by the American Law Institute, are not themselves primary authority, they are often cited and quoted in judicial opinions. When this occurs and the court adopts the restatement rule, it effectively becomes primary authority – but only because of the court's appropriation of it.

Restatements are available only for the following areas of the law: Agency; Conflict of Laws; Contracts; Foreign Relations; Judgments; Property; Restitution; Security; Torts; Trusts; and Unfair Competition.

The restatements are very poorly indexed. There is no general index to the entire set. Each individual restatement has its own index. If the restatement appears in multiple volumes, it may lack an index to the restatement as a whole, requiring users to consult the separate index of each volume.

Each restatement also has a series of appendix volumes, arranged by restatement number, that provide citations to cases that have applied the restatement.

B. The West Publishing Company and Its Reporters

The quasi-secondary editorial content found in digests and annotated codes provides a wealth of information to the researcher and allows researchers to compile in short order a list of citations to primary legal authorities relating to their issues. To put digests and codes in their proper perspective, it is helpful to know a little about one of their chief progenitors, the West Publishing Company and the case reporters it produces.

1. Background of the West Publishing Company

In the late 1800s, John West, a law book salesman, recognized that legal research was ineffective and inefficient for a variety of reasons. At that time, most statutory codes and the reporters that printed the decisions of courts were published by the states themselves or by their agents. They rarely appeared in a timely fashion and little uniformity of presentation existed between the outputs of different jurisdictions. Legal research was further hampered by a lack of case-finding aids, and the statutory codes provided few, if any, links to the cases that applied them.

West addressed the problems confronting researchers in two ways. He published a national system of reporters that reprinted the decisions of the principal national and state courts. These reporters were distinguished by their timeliness and uniformity of presentation. West's reporters also featured what West called a "topic and key number system," an ingenious classification scheme that provided the linkage between related primary authorities that, theretofore, researchers had so sorely lacked.

2. West's Topic and Key Number System

West's topic and key number system classified cases by their subject matter, thereby making them accessible through keyword searching. Publications called digests became the vehicle through which that searching was performed and the citations to related cases presented.

The West system currently breaks the law down into over 440 major subject categories called "topics," arranged in alphabetical order, e.g.:

- Abandoned & Lost Property

- Abatement & Revival

- Abortion & Birth Control

Each topic, in turn, is broken down into subtopics, numbered by Roman numerals, which relate to different aspects of the major topic. These subtopics, in turn, are broken down into sub-subtopics. Each sub-subtopic is assigned a so-called "key number" in sequential order. For example, what follows is a portion of the breakdown of the topic "Abatement & Revival:"

I. Objections to Jurisdiction

Key # 1. Want of jurisdiction as grounds for abandonment.

Key # 2. Jurisdiction of the person.

Key # 3. Necessity and mode of making the objection.

II. Another Action Pending

Key # 4. Ground of abatement in general.

Key # 5. Nature of other action or proceeding.

3. West's Headnotes

Every reported case is read by a West editor. The editor determines the points of law the case addresses and writes a so-called "headnote" for each point. Each headnote includes an assigned topic and key number from the West classification scheme in accordance with the point's subject matter; a short description of the point; and, if applicable, a citation to a statute to which the point relates.

The following is an example of a West headnote:

Abatement & Revival [key symbol] 4

Statute precluding assertion of claim in the Claims Court if a suit is pending in the district court on a tort claim with the same operative facts does not apply to district courts or to boards of contract appeals and does not preclude assertion of contract claim before a board while a tort claim is being pursued in district court. 28 U.S.C.A. § 1500.

Headnotes and their associated topic and key numbers enable the creation of a network of linked research tools, which facilitate the gathering of cases and statutes related to a particular point of law. The chief components of this network are reporters, digests, and annotated statutory codes.

4. West's Reporters

A reporter is a collection of the opinions of the courts of either a single jurisdiction or multiple jurisdictions, chronologically arranged by the dates of their decisions. Although there were many reporters printing judicial opinions before John West came along, his innovation was to develop a system of reporters, covering most jurisdictions, which printed cases in a timely and uniform manner and that tied them into his topic and key number system.

The West reporter system is called a national reporter system because its constituent reporters cover the federal courts and the courts of all 50 states. The following table ties the components of the West national reporter system to the jurisdictions and courts they cover.

West Federal Court Reporters

Supreme Court Reporter	United States Supreme Court
Federal Reporter	United States Circuit Courts of Appeals
Federal Supplement	United States District Courts
Federal Rules & Decisions	United States District Court decisions (not in the Federal Supplement) related to the Federal Rules of Civil Procedure, Federal Rules of Criminal Procedure, Federal Rules of Appellate Procedure, and the Federal Rules of Evidence.
Bankruptcy Reporter	United States Bankruptcy Courts, United States Bankruptcy Appellate Panels, and bankruptcy-related decisions from other federal courts.

West Regional Reporters

Atlantic Reporter	Appellate Courts of CT, DE, DC, ME, MD, NH, NJ, PA, RI, VT
North Eastern Reporter	Appellate Courts of IL, IN, MA, NY, OH
North Western Reporter	Appellate Courts of IA, MI, MN, NE, ND, SD, WI
South Eastern Reporter	Appellate Courts of GA, NC, SC, VA, WV
Southern Reporter	Appellate Courts of AL, FL, LA, MS
South Western Reporter	Appellate Courts of AR, KY, MO, TN, TX
Pacific Reporter	Appellate Courts of AK, AZ, CA, CO, HI, ID, KS, MT, NV, NM, OK, OR, UT, WA, WY

West Individual State Reporters

These reporters reprint the appellate decisions of a single state in chronological order by date of decision. Around 30 of these single-state reporters are currently published. They are sometimes called "offprint reporters" because they retain the same volume numbers and pagination as the regional reporters. To achieve this conformity, gaps frequently appear in the page sequences of offprint reporters.

5. The Components of an Opinion in a West Reporter

Opinions in West reporters include features that aid researchers in multiple ways.

a. Parallel Citations

It is not uncommon for the decision of a case to be reported in different reporters. Parallel citations are the citations to that case in those different reporters. They are parallel in the sense that they refer to the same decision published in a different place. If a decision has such parallel citations, they will appear at the top of the entry for the decision in the West reporter.

b. Syllabus

The syllabus is an overview of the holding of the case, which is written by an editor at West. It appears after the name of the case and provides a snapshot of its holding that researchers use to determine its initial relevance. The syllabus, however, is not part of the opinion itself and should never be quoted and/or cited in legal writing.

c. Headnotes

As noted above, the editors at West write a headnote that summarizes each point of law the case discusses. The headnotes precede the opinion in a West reporter and are numbered consecutively. These consecutively bracketed numbers, [1], [2], etc., should not be confused with the topic and key number that is also assigned to each headnote. Like the syllabus, headnotes are read by researchers as an initial introduction to the case. West also helps researchers locate the specific parts of the opinion to which the headnotes relate.

Within the opinion, the bracketed headnote numbers appear at the places where discussion of the corresponding points of law begin.

The topic and key number, which follows each bracketed headnote number, alerts researchers to the place in the digest where this headnote and related headnotes from other cases are collected. Knowing the topic and key number, the researcher is able to go directly into the digest to locate additional cases, bypassing the need to consult the descriptive word and other indexes that provide topic and key number references.

6. West Digests

A digest is a case-finding tool for the jurisdiction or court to which it relates. To illustrate how a digest works, let's take a state digest as an example. That digest arranges in West topic and key number order the West headnotes written initially for inclusion in the West regional reporter encompassing the state's judicial opinions. When a researcher turns to a particular topic and key number in the digest, all of the headnotes from the state's cases that were assigned that topic and key number will be grouped together, creating a list of cases of like subject matter. Moreover, because every headnote includes the case's citation and a summary of its holding on the point at hand, the researcher can easily identify and retrieve the cases of the greatest potential interest to him or her.

West publishes a wide array of digests. Some relate to particular courts and others to specific jurisdictions. Every jurisdiction is covered by at least one digest.

The following table illustrates their multiplicity and scope:

West Digests

Decennial Digest	Incorporates materials from all West digests at ten-year intervals
U.S. Supreme Court Reports Digest	United States Supreme Court
Federal Digest	United States Supreme Court, United States Circuit Courts of Appeals, and United States District Courts
Bankruptcy Digest	United States Bankruptcy Courts, bankruptcy decisions of the United States District Courts, United States Courts of Appeals, and the United States Supreme Court, as well as bankruptcy points of law from state courts
Atlantic Digest	Appellate courts from CT, DE, DC, ME, MD, NH, NJ, PA, RI, VT
North Western Digest	Appellate courts from IA, MI, MN, NE, ND, SD, WI
Pacific Digest	Appellate courts from AK, AZ, CA, CO, HI, ID, KS, MT, NV, NM, OK, OR, UT, WA, WY
South Eastern Digest	Appellate courts from GA, NC, SC, VA, WV

To find relevant cases in a West digest, the researcher must know the topic and key numbers to which his or her issues relate. Several indexes at the back of each set of West digests provide this information.

a. Descriptive Word Index

The Descriptive Word Index is a keyword index that links words and concepts to their related topic and key numbers.

b. Words and Phrases

Words and Phrases lists in alphabetical order commonly used legal words and phrases with links to their related topic and key numbers.

7. Annotated Codes

A code is a compilation of a jurisdiction's statutes, presented in a subject arrangement determined by the jurisdiction. An official code is a code published by the jurisdiction, itself. The United States Code is an example of such an official code.

An annotated code is a version of a jurisdiction's code published by a commercial publisher. Annotated codes conform to the organization of each jurisdiction's official code and reprint the texts of the statutes exactly as they appear in those official versions. If a jurisdiction has no official code, the annotated code will nonetheless follow an organization determined by the jurisdiction.

A number of factors distinguish annotated codes from official codes. Annotated codes tend to be issued and updated more frequently. Updating occurs variously through the issuance of pocket parts, by the publication of supplements in separate volumes, or by a new edition of the code. In addition, annotated codes typically include value-added features to aid the researcher, as listed in the following table.

Features of Annotated Codes

Historical and Statutory Notes	Outline the legislative history of the statute from its adoption through any subsequent amendments. The coverage is often more extensive than that found in related sections of official codes.
Cross References	Refer users to related (and perhaps more relevant) sections of the code.
Library References	List pertinent secondary source materials, including treatises and law review articles.
Notes of Decisions	The most useful feature of the annotated code, apart from the text of the code itself. Notes of Decisions cite and briefly describe the cases that have applied each code section. The list is organized by topic so that related cases appear together. When the list of cases is very extensive, a mini keyword index appears at the beginning of Notes of Decisions to aid the researcher in finding the topic of greatest benefit to him or her. Each entry includes the name of the case, the court, the date of decision, the reporter citation, and a brief description of the holding of the case.
General Index	Appears at the end of the annotated code in multiple paperback volumes, which are updated and published annually. The index is an alphabetical, key-word subject index that provides references to the statutory sections to which the terms relate. The statutory citation generally employs abbreviations. Tables explaining the abbreviations typically appear at the beginning of the index or in the introductory materials to the code.
Popular Names Table	Lists alphabetically the names by which statutes are commonly known and directs users to their place in the code. These tables generally follow the General Index, either as a separate volume at the end of the set or as an addition to the last volume of the General Index.

West's *United States Code Annotated* provides up-to-date coverage of the federal code. West also publishes annotated codes for all 50 states and the District of Columbia. The electronic versions of these West annotated codes are available on Westlaw. In Texas, West publishes *Vernon's Texas Statutes and Codes Annotated* (the current code arrangement) and *Vernon's Texas Revised Civil Statutes Annotated* (the mostly, but not entirely, superseded code arrangement), as well as annotated versions of the Business Corporation Act, Code of Criminal Procedure, Insurance Code, and Probate Code.

United States Code Service, published by the rival legal publisher, Michie, provides researchers an alternative annotated federal code to West's *United States Code Annotated*. Because *United States Code Service* is produced by a different publisher and editorial team, its publishing schedule, annotations, and other reference content are unique to it. *United States Code Service* is available electronically on Lexis.

Step 6: Use fee-based legal databases to retrieve authorities by citation and employ citators to verify they remain good law.

After relevant authorities have been identified using non-fee-based secondary authorities and quasi-secondary editorial materials in paper digests, annotated codes, and reporters, it is time to retrieve what has been found. Although a researcher could accomplish this in paper sources, the time saved using electronic databases, such as Lexis, Westlaw, and Bloomberg Law makes them a better option, notwithstanding their attendant user costs. This is particularly true because, by approaching these databases with citations to known authorities already in hand, we can minimize the costs of their use.

A. Locating Documents by Citation

Lexis, Westlaw, and Bloomberg Law permit users to enter a citation to an authority in a designated search box on their home screens.

1. Retrieving Cases

Neither Lexis, Westlaw, nor Bloomberg Law requires that the citation be complete or in proper Bluebook form. A user need only input the volume, the reporter abbreviation, and the first page of the case. For example, *Smith v. Jones*, 72 F.2d 356 (2d Cir. 1985) could be input simply as "72 F.2d 356".

a. Retrieving Cases in WestlawNext

Follow these steps to retrieve cases in WestlawNext:

1. Enter the case citation in the general search box at the top of the main screen. Click Search.

2. The full text of the case appears. Scan it for relevance.

b. Retrieving Cases in Westlaw Classic

Follow these steps to retrieve cases in Westlaw Classic:

1. Locate the Find by Citation box on the main search screen, input the case citation, and click Go.

2. The full text of the case appears at the right of the screen. Scan the opinion for relevance.

c. Retrieving Cases in Lexis Advance

Follow these steps to retrieve cases in Lexis Advance:

1. Enter the case citation in the general search box at the top of the main search screen. Click Search.

2. The full text of the case appears. Scan the opinion for relevance.

d. Retrieving Cases in Lexis.com

Follow these steps to retrieve cases in Lexis.com:

1. Find the Quick Tools section at the right of the main search screen, input the case citation in the box below, and click Get a Doc.

2. The full text of the case appears. Scan the opinion for relevance.

e. Retrieving Cases in Bloomberg Law

Follow these steps to retrieve cases in Bloomberg Law:

1. Enter the case citation in the Find cases, news, companies, people and more... box at the upper right of the home screen.

2. The full text of the case appears. Scan the opinion for relevance.

2. Retrieving Statutes

Statutory citations cannot be input as intuitively as cases. Fortunately, Lexis.com, WestlawNext, Westlaw Classic, and Bloomberg Law provide templates to guide the user. Lexis Advance does not.

a. Using the Statutory Templates in WestlawNext

Follow these steps to use the statutory templates in WestlawNext:

1. Under Browse on the homepage, click Statutes and Court Rules.

2. Click the jurisdiction on the Statutes and Court Rules page.

3. At Statutes Find Template, locate the appropriate statutory title, insert the section number, and click Go.

4. The full text of the statute appears. Scan it for relevance.

b. Retrieving Statutes by Citation in WestlawClassic

Follow these steps to retrieve statutes by citation in WestlawClassic:

1. To access the United States Code Annotated template: type "usca" in the Find by Citation box on the main search screen.

2. To access state code templates, type the two-letter state abbreviation followed by a space and "st" in the

Find by Citation box on the main search screen. For example, to locate the template for the Texas code, type "TX st".

3. When the template appears, fill in the required information and click Go.

4. The full text of statute appears. Scan it for relevance.

c. Retrieving Federal Statutes by Citation in Lexis Advance

Follow these steps to retrieve federal statutes by citation in Lexis Advance:

1. There are no statutory templates per se in Lexis Advance.

2. In the general search box at the top of the home screen, type the title number, "uscs", and the section number. For example, Section 934 of Title 10 of the United States Codes would be input as "10 uscs 934".

3. The full text of the statute appears. Scan it for relevance.

4. Click the table of contents box at the left to see surrounding code sections.

d. Retrieving State Statutes by Citation in Lexis Advance

Follow these steps to retrieve state statutes by citation in Lexis Advance:

1. In the general search box at the top of the home screen, type the state name, the name of the code, and the section number. For example, Section 21.051 of the

Texas Labor Code would be input as "Texas Labor 21.051".

2. A list of search results appears at the right. Look at the Narrow column at the left. Under Content Type, click Codes.

3. Review the summaries of the search results. The result for the code should be at or near the top. Click on it to retrieve the full text and scan the statute for relevance.

e. Retrieving Federal Statutes by Citation in Lexis.com

Follow these steps to retrieve federal statutes by citation in Lexis.com:

1. Find the Quick Tools section at the right of the main search screen. In the box below, input the statutory citation in the form "title number U.S.C.S. section number". Click Get a Doc.

2. The full text of the statute appears. Scan the opinion for relevance.

f. Using the State Statutory Templates in Lexis.com

Follow these steps to use the state statutory templates in Lexis.com:

1. Find States Legal – U.S. on the home page.

2. Click on the desired state.

3. Under Quick Tools at the upper right of the screen, click Get a document by cite.

4. Fill in the blanks in the Statute template and click Go.

5. The full text appears. Scan the statute for relevance.

g. Using the Federal Statutory Templates in Bloomberg Law

Follow these steps to use the federal statutory templates in Bloomberg Law:

1. Under Getting Started/Research, click Federal Law.

2. Click Federal Legislative.

3. Click United States Code (USC).

4. Find the desired title in the list of titles and click the plus sign to its left.

5. Click Expand next level.

6. Click on the desired section.

h. Using the State Statutory Templates in Bloomberg Law

Follow these steps to use the state statutory templates in Bloomberg Law:

1. Under Getting Started/Research, click State Law. On the next screen, click the desired state on the map of the United States.

2. Click [State] Legislative.

3. Click [State] Statutes.

4. Find the desired title/subject/ article and click the plus sign to its left.

5. Click Expand next level.

6. Continue clicking Expand Next Level until the section breakdown appears.

7. Click on the desired section.

B. Use Citators to Determine Whether an Authority Is Good Law

As soon as a primary authority has been retrieved, the researcher should use the database's citator to verify that it remains good law. An attorney's time is simply too precious and too costly to justify his or her attention to an authority that has no legal standing. Citators are mechanisms that provide attorneys a general indication of the current legal status of cases, statutes, regulations, and decisions of administrative law courts. Although most comprehensive legal databases include a citator (Google Scholar being the notable exception), Lexis' citator, Shepard's, and Westlaw's citator, KeyCite, are the most established and widely used. Bloomberg Law's BCite performs similar functions.

Citators can be accessed from the providers' main search pages. The researcher simply types the citation of the primary authority for which information is sought in a designated box. Citators can also be accessed directly from the full-text version of an authority by means of a variety of links. If the researcher has already retrieved the authority by citation, he or she is most likely to access the citator from these full-text links.

When the authority is a case, Lexis, Westlaw, and Bloomberg Law place a signal next to the case name at the top of the text. The signal alerts the reader immediately to potential problems concerning the case's legal status. In Lexis, various iconic signals indicate whether the decision has received positive, negative, cautionary, or neutral treatment in subsequent court decisions. Westlaw, on the other hand, appends a red flag to warn that the case is no longer good law for at least one of its legal points and a yellow flag to indicate that, while the case has not yet been reversed or overruled, some negative treatment exists. Clicking on the symbol takes the researcher directly into the citator. Bloomberg Law employs green and red signals to signify positive or negative treatment.

No trained researcher rejects a case simply on the basis of the signal it has received. The signals merely express the opinions of the editors at Shepard's, KeyCite, and Bloomberg Law and are not infallible. The treatment of cases is often in the eye of the beholder. Sometimes, Shephard's or KeyCite or Bloomberg Law just get it wrong. And, most importantly, the negative treatment signals do not indicate what part of the case was treated negatively by the subsequent court. It is not uncommon for courts to reject one aspect of a case while leaving others aspects untouched. If one has any doubt why negative treatment symbols should be treated with extreme caution, consider the following scenario: The same negative treatment symbol will be appended to a case in which only a minor facet was subsequently overruled as to a case that was overruled in its entirety. Likewise, a case may receive a negative treatment symbol when it has been treated harshly by the decision of a court outside the jurisdiction, which has no bearing on the validity of the ruling within the initial jurisdiction. For all of these reasons, attorneys have an ethical duty to go beyond the symbols and read the supposedly negative decisions to determine for themselves their legal impact.

Citators, in general, are organized into two basic categories: history and citing authorities.

1. History

The History category identifies any prior or subsequent actions that occurred directly in relation to the same litigation or proceeding. It would include, for example, the citation of the appellate court decision that affirmed or reversed the trial court decision in a particular case.

The information in the History category is obviously critical in determining the status of any given authority as good law. It is also used in case citation. For example, the Bluebook requires that any subsequent case history be appended to the initial citation of a case. The writ or petition history that the Greenbook requires in citations of Texas Court of Appeals cases is also located in the History categories of citators. Finally, although the prior history of cases is not usually cited, it can be helpful to researchers who may find in earlier decisions additional factual information about relevant cases.

2. Citing Authorities

The Citing Authorities segment lists citations of authorities that have cited the known authority. The Citing Authorities category incorporates primary authorities from various jurisdictions. These include negative citing authorities that may have overruled or otherwise invalidated the initial authority. The Citing Authorities category also includes selected secondary authorities and legal briefs that have cited the initial authority.

Each citation on the list of Citing Authorities includes an explanation of the treatment the initial authority received. For example, the explanation may indicate whether the initial authority was approved, criticized, or distinguished. The citation may also explain the depth of treatment accorded to the initial authority, indicating the degree of detail in which the authority was discussed. It should not be assumed, however, that the depth of treatment is necessarily indicative of the usefulness of the authority.

The list of Citing Authorities can be filtered by jurisdiction or kinds of treatment. It can also be limited to citations of materials addressing topics related to particular headnotes in the full text of the original opinion.

Obviously, the researcher needs to review any citing authority that purportedly overrules or supersedes the authority he or she proposes to use. Critical or distinguishing citing authorities from the prevailing jurisdiction should also be analyzed as they may indicate developing trends in the interpretation of the law, which must be understood to properly predict the law's consequences or argue its effects.

3. Using Citators

a. Shepardizing in Lexis.com

Follow these steps to Shepardize in Lexis.com:

1. Find the Quick Tools box at the right of the home screen. Enter the citation and click Shepardize.

2. Alternatively, if a document already has been pulled up in full text, click on the icon next to the authority's name or on the Shepard's box at the top of the screen.

3. Review the Shepard's Summary. It alerts the researcher to prior or subsequent history. If such history is present, it appears below the summary. Texas writ and petition history will appear in the history segment. When negative subsequent history is present, clicking the citation brings it on-screen. Read the subsequent authority to determine the respects in which it is negative. If it upends the initial citation, use it as the basis of future research.

4. Note whether there are citing decisions. These are additional sources of primary authority to cull. Several different mechanisms facilitate the review of citing decisions:

- Shepard's Summary breaks down the citing decisions by treatment or type. Clicking on any given category brings up a list of the related citations. Shepard's Summary also categorizes the citing decisions by the Lexis headnotes to which they relate. Clicking on any given headnote brings up a list of the related citing cases.
- FOCUS-Restrict By is located at the top of the screen. It facilitates the filtering of cases by kind of treatment, kind of opinion (concurring or dissenting), jurisdiction, headnote number, date, and by terms specified by the user.

b. Shepardizing in Lexis Advance

Follow these steps to Shepardize in Lexis Advance:

1. Input the citation in the main search box on the research screen.

2. Click on the Shepard's icon next to the document title on the full-text screen. Alternately, click on the "Shepardize® this document" link in the Shepard's column at the upper right of the screen.

3. For cases, the Appellate History screen appears, providing the direct history of the proceeding. Texas writ or petition history will be noted here as will citations to decisions that affirmed or reversed a decision on appeal.

4. Other categories of Shepard's include:

   - Citing Decisions cites cases that have cited the document. A decision that has overruled the

Shepardized case will be cited here. The results can be restricted using the prompts in the Narrow By column at the left of the screen. Results can be narrowed by kind of treatment, jurisdiction, headnote number, specified terms, and date.

- Other Citing Sources cites law reviews, treatises, and other secondary sources that have cited the document. The results can also be restricted by prompts in the Narrow By column at the left of the screen. Results can be narrowed by content type, specified terms, and date.

5. Use the prompts in the Narrow By column at the left of the screen to filter results by content type, specified terms, and date.

c. KeyCiting in WestlawNext

Follow these steps to KeyCite in WestlawNext:

1. Input the citation in the main search box on the research screen to retrieve the document.

2. Boxes with links to various categories of KeyCite appear above the title of the document.

3. Clicking on the History box leads to a list of prior or subsequent history in the same litigation or proceeding. Texas writ or petition history will appear here as will citations to cases that affirmed or reversed a decision on appeal.

4. Clicking on the Negative Treatment box leads to a list of decisions that treated the authority negatively. Citations to overruling cases will appear here.

5. Clicking on the Citing References box leads to a list of materials that have cited the authority. These may include secondary sources in addition to primary authorities, which have cited the authority.

6. The View box at the upper left of the KeyCite screen divides the citing authorities by category. Clicking on any given category leads to a list of the related citing references. The user can further restrict the results using the filtering commands located in the Narrow column at the lower left.

   • The results can be restricted to those containing terms specified by the user or by jurisdiction, date, depth of treatment, headnote topics, treatment status, and/or publication status.

   • The entire list of results can be restricted by inputting terms in the Search within results" box on the initial Citing References screen, located at the left under Narrow.

d. KeyCiting in Westlaw Classic

Follow these steps to KeyCite in Westlaw Classic:

1. Input the citation in the KeyCite this Citation box at the left of the main search screen.

2. Alternatively, if the full text is already on the screen, the KeyCite links appear at the top of the left-hand column.

3. The Full History link includes any direct prior or subsequent history. Texas writ or petition history will appear here as will citations to cases that affirmed or reversed a decision on appeal. Full History also includes negative citing references in different proceedings. Citations to overruling opinions will appear here.

4. Direct History (graphical view) presents the prior and subsequent history of the proceeding in a schematic diagram.

5. Citing References lists citations to primary and secondary authorities, which have cited the initial authority. Primary citing references precede secondary citing references. Primary citing references are organized first by kinds of treatment, then by depth of treatment, and finally by jurisdiction.

6. The Limit KeyCite Display box appears at the bottom left of the full text. Clicking it leads to a filtering screen where the user may restrict the KeyCite listings by document type, jurisdiction, and headnote number.

7. The locate link allows the user to specify particular text that must appear in the citing results.

e. BCiting in Bloomberg Law

Follow these steps to BCite in Bloomberg Law:

1. Input the citation in in the Find cases, news, companies, people and more... box at the upper right of the home screen.

2. The BCite Categories appear at the top of the case.

3. Click Direct History for citations to prior and subsequent history of this case.

4. Click Case Analysis to determine whether the case remains good law and to determine the reactions of subsequent courts to it. Use the filters at the left of the screen to filter by citing case analysis, citing case status, citation frequency, court, judge, date, etc.

5. Click Table of Authorities for a list of the cases cited by the case.

6. Click Citing Documents for a list of documents citing the case. Use the filters at the left of the screen to filter by content type and date.

Step 7: Follow the links found in the authorities retrieved in fee-based legal databases to locate additional sources, effectively employing those databases more as suppliers of known authority than as initial law-finders.

Once a relevant legal authority has been confirmed as good law, it is time to use that authority as the source from which all or almost all other authorities related to the issue will be obtained. With that authority in hand, all of the benefits of the electronic databases can be utilized while avoiding the costly pitfalls of keyword subject searching. As noted, keyword searching is time-consuming and frustrating if one is unsure of the appropriate keywords. It also tends to be the most expensive kind of searching to perform.

The integrated approach that lies at the heart of this research strategy, which combines initial research in no-fee sources with later use of Lexis, Westlaw, or Bloomberg Law, is generally the most effective in terms of the results gathered and the time and costs saved. Beginning a subject search in no-fee secondary sources, particularly in paper, takes full advantage of indexing features, which guide even the most clueless researchers to relevant materials and those all-essential citations. With these citations in hand, researchers can then use Lexis, Westlaw, and Bloomberg Law to retrieve the materials themselves and, by following the links appended to and contained within these materials, unlock nearly everything else of relevance to their issues with the least cost.

Relevance and cost are the critical concepts that underlie this strategy. Increasingly, Lexis and Westlaw are adopting fee structures that bill not for the initial search, but rather for every search result that is viewed. Thus, every click on a search result that proves fruitless is essentially money down the drain. And, at $15 or $20 a click (which is at the lowest end of the pricing scale), ill-advised clicks quickly add up to serious money. On the other hand, Bloomberg Law provides unlimited searching and reading of results as part of its standard package.

Regardless of the provider's pricing model, researchers have far greater assurance that the results will be relevant and to the point if they approach Lexis, Westlaw, or Bloomberg Law with a citation of known relevance and use it as the source of all that follows. Moreover, because their research results will be so much more targeted than the results of a general keyword search, researchers are spared the time and trouble of poring over long lists of results to separate the wheat from the chaff. Indeed, the known citation approach to legal research almost always produces pure wheat and does so very quickly.

This section will first explain in general terms the common features of the electronic providers, which make it possible to assemble all of this information from a single citation. It will then provide step-by-step guidance in using the specific features of Lexis, Westlaw, and Bloomberg Law to achieve these results.

A. Common Features of Lexis, Westlaw, and Bloomberg Law

To grasp how one citation can unlock all of the legal authority pertaining to the legal issue you are researching, you need to understand the core finding tools adopted by the providers of electronic legal information and how they work. Fortunately, the systems of these major providers are quite similar in terms of their formats and applications.

1. Internal Links

Most primary and secondary legal authorities cite other legal authorities. In Lexis, Westlaw, and Bloomberg Law, clicking on a cited authority will take you to that authority. That authority, in turn, will cite additional authorities, which can be viewed by clicking on their links. Those authorities also cite additional authorities, which are just a click away. By following the internal links, researchers can quickly assemble a comprehensive body of law relating directly to their issues.

2. Headnotes

West's topic and key number system and its associated case headnotes are fully integrated into Westlaw. Lexis, in turn, has created its own headnotes and linked them to a classification scheme of its own devising. Unfortunately, one cannot move readily from one classification system to the other. Although both Westlaw's and Lexis's systems provide comprehensive coverage of the key subjects of the law, they are completely different in the way they are organized. Thus, knowing an issue's applicable West topic and key number is of no value when using Lexis.

Westlaw and Lexis headnotes are also created differently. Whereas a West headnote is a summary of a point of law written by a human editor, a Lexis headnote is generated electronically and replicates a portion of the actual text from the opinion. This difference is of no significance if one enters either system with a citation in hand, as is being done now. The difference, though, could matter more in keyword subject searches where the headnotes and other editorial enhancements are searched as well as the text. For example, suppose that a West editor used a word that did not actually appear in the opinion itself in the West headnote he or she composed for a particular case. A search using the word on Westlaw would capture that case. On the other hand, a search using the same word on Lexis would not, since Lexis headnotes are drawn purely from the text in which that word does not actually appear.

Headnotes are an important tool when research is begun with a known citation. When one pulls up a case by its citation, the respective headnotes appear at the top before the opinion. Both Lexis and Westlaw allow the researcher to use any given headnote as a point of access into their respective classification systems. By clicking on a link adjacent to the headnote, the researcher is presented with a list of cases that relate to the same point of law. In effect, the reader enters into an electronic version of a digest. These virtual digests offer yet another way of harvesting additional citations from the initial citation.

Bloomberg Law, on the other hand, has not yet developed a comprehensive headnote system. However, some linkage of related materials exists through the topical scheme employed by the BNA publications in the Bloomberg Law database.

3. Citators

Citators like Shepard's in Lexis and KeyCite in Westlaw and BCite in Bloomberg Law already have been discussed as updating tools that help researchers determine whether primary authorities remain good law. However, citators are equally useful as mechanisms for gathering additional authorities from a citation to a known authority. The Citing Authorities segments of citators are a researcher's godsend. As noted, they provide citations to cases, law review articles, ALR annotations, and other primary and secondary sources that have cited the known authority. Accordingly, citators make locating additional, relevant materials very easy. Even if good authorities already have been found, a review of the Citing Authorities or Citing References is essential as it may bring to light authorities that are even better in terms of jurisdiction, depth of treatment, and/or factual relevance. Citing Authorities can also provide links to the very latest materials, which otherwise could easily escape notice.

B. Researching in WestlawNext from a Single Citation

1. Using a Case Cite

Follow these steps for every case you encounter:

1. Type the initial case citation in the search box on the home screen.

2. Scan the case to verify its relevance.

3. KeyCite the case as discussed in Step 6.

4. If the case remains good law, read it carefully.

5. Note other authorities cited within each case. Click on the internal links to pull them up. If the authority is a statute, follow the instructions for researching from statutory cites.

6. Review the headnotes to each case. Click on the topics and key numbers of pertinent headnotes of each case to go to the digest to find other cases with headnotes having the same topics and key numbers.

7. Click on the "Cases that cite this headnote" link under a relevant headnote. This provides the KeyCite citing references to the case, which relate to the topic of the headnote.

8. Click on the authority to pull it up. Scan the case for relevance.

2. Using a Statutory Cite

Follow these steps for every statute you encounter:

1. Type the initial statutory citation in the search box on the home screen.

2. Scan the statute to verify its relevance.

3. KeyCite the statute as discussed in Step 6.

4. If the statute remains good law, read it carefully.

5. Check the Notes of Decisions. Review the topical index at the beginning of the Notes of Decisions to find the sections relating to the research topic. Follow up cites to pertinent cases as discussed above.

C. Researching in Westlaw Classic from a Single Citation

1. Using a Case Cite

Follow these steps for every case you encounter:

1. Type the initial case citation in the Find by Citation box on the home screen.

2. Scan the case to verify its relevance.

3. KeyCite the case as discussed in Step 6.

4. If the case remains good law, read it carefully.

5. Note other authorities cited within each case. Click on the internal links to pull them up. If the authority is a statute, follow the instructions for researching from statutory cites.

6. Review the headnotes to each case. Click on the topics and key numbers of pertinent headnotes of each case. Use the Custom Digest to filter the digest entries retrieved by jurisdiction, search term, or date.

7. Consult the Citing References segment of the KeyCite entry for each case.

8. Click on the authority to pull it up. Scan the case to verify its relevance.

2. Using a Statutory Cite

Follow these steps for every statute you encounter:

1. Type the initial statutory citation in the Find by Citation box on the home screen.

2. Scan the statute to verify its relevance.

3. KeyCite the statute as discussed in Step 6.

4. If the statute remains good law, read it carefully.

5. Check the Notes of Decisions. Follow up cites to pertinent cases as discussed above.

D. Researching in Lexis Advance from a Single Citation

1. Using a Case Cite

Follow these steps for every case you encounter:

1. Type the initial case citation in the search box on the home screen.

2. Scan the case to verify its relevance.

3. Shepardize the case as discussed in Step 6.

4. If the case remains good law, read it carefully.

5. Note other authorities cited within each case. Click on the internal links to pull them up. If the authority is a statute, follow the instructions for researching from statutory cites.

6. Click the Activate Passages link in the right column of the screen. The text of the decision will be divided into boxes relating to particular points of law discussed in the case. Double-click anywhere in a relevant box (except on an existing link). A list of cases cited by this case and of cases citing this case for this issue appears.

7. Review the headnotes to each case. Find pertinent headnotes. Links to their related digest topics and subtopics appear above each headnote. Click on the link at the end of the string, then click Get Documents to retrieve cases assigned the same topic and subtopic in Lexis's electronic digest. Use the filters in the left column to customize the results by type of material, jurisdiction, date, and inclusion of keywords.

8. A link titled Shepardize – Narrow By This Headnote appears beside each headnote. Clicking on this link leads to a list of the Citing Authorities from Shepard's that cited the case in relation to the subject matter of the headnote.

9. Alternatively, consult the Citing Authorities of the segment of the Shepard's entry for each case. Click on the authority to pull it up.

10. Click on Topic Summaries/View Reports in the right column of the screen. A list of topics related to the case appears. Clicking on a desired topic leads to an overview of the issue with citations to leading primary and secondary authorities. Links to materials from other jurisdictions appear in the column at the right.

2. Using a Statutory Cite

Follow these steps for every statute you encounter:

1. Type the initial statutory citation in the search box on the home screen.

2. Scan the statute to verify its relevance.

3. Shepardize the case as discussed in Step 6.

4. If the statute remains good law, read it carefully.

5. Click the Table of Contents tab at the left to see where the statute lies in the Code and its surrounding sections.

6. Check the Case Notes at the end of the statute for summaries of cases applying the statute. The Case Notes are ordered by topic. A list of the topics appears at the beginning. Review the list to find a relevant topic.

Click on the blue arrow at the left of any given topic to be taken directly to its related cases. Pull up relevant cases by their citation as discussed above.

7. Click the Expert Analysis link in the right column at the beginning of the statute to retrieve secondary authorities discussing aspects of the statute.

8. Click Topic Summaries/View Reports in the right column at the beginning of the statute to see a list of reports on related topics. Each report includes a list of seminal cases.

E. Researching in Lexis.com from a Single Citation

1. Using a Case Cite

Follow these steps for every case you encounter:

1. Type the initial case citation in the search box on the home screen.

2. Scan the case to verify its relevance.

3. Shepardize the case as discussed in Step 6.

4. If the case remains good law, read it carefully.

5. Note other authorities cited within each case. Click on the internal links to pull them up. If the authority is a statute, follow the instructions for researching from statutory cites.

6. Review the headnotes to each case. Click the More Like This Headnote link of pertinent headnotes to go to the digest to find other cases with similar headnotes.

7. Consult the Citing Authorities segment of the Shepard's entry for each case. Click on the authority to pull it up.

2. Using a Statutory Cite

Follow these steps for every statute you encounter:

1. Type the initial statutory citation in the search box on the home screen.

2. Scan the statute to verify its relevance.

3. Shepardize the statute as discussed in Step 6.

4. If the statute remains good law, read it carefully.

5. Check the Interpretive Notes and Decisions. Follow up cites to pertinent cases as discussed above.

F. Researching in Bloomberg Law from a Single Citation.

1. Using a Case Cite

Follow these steps for every case you encounter:

1. Input the citation in in the "Find cases, news, companies, people and more…" box at the upper right of the home screen.

2. BCite the case by clicking the Direct History and Case Analysis tabs at the top of the screen.

3. If the case remains good law, read it carefully.

4. Note other authorities cited within the case. Click on the internal links to pull them up.

5. Click Table of Authorities for a list of the cases cited by the case.

6. Click Citing Opinions for a list of cases citing the case. Use the filters at the left of the screen to filter by content type and date.

7. Click on a citing authority to pull it up. Scan the case to verify its relevance.

2. Using a Statutory Cite

Follow these steps for every statute you encounter:

1. Enter the statutory citation in the Find cases, news, companies, people and more... box at the upper right of the home screen. The citation must be in U.S.C. form. Bloomberg Law does not access U.S.C.A. or U.S.C.S. citations.

2. Click Go. The full text of the statute appears. Scan it for relevance.

3. Click the Case Analysis tab at the top of the statute.

4. Use the filters at the left of the screen to filter the results by a keyword search of the cases' extracts (descriptions), keyword search of the cases' full text, date, strength of discussion, court, topic, etc.

5. Pull up and read relevant cases. Follow their internal links and BCite them to find additional cases.

Step 8: If research must be initiated in fee-based legal databases through keyword subject searches, perform those searches carefully and wisely.

Since the object of the research strategy discussed here is to avoid initiating legal research through keyword subject searches in fee-based legal databases such as Lexis and Westlaw, the reader may rightfully assume that this step has been included with a certain lack of enthusiasm. Indeed, the decision to begin with a costly subject search in these databases seems particularly unjustified considering that every practitioner with access to them presumably can also access the internet. Although the internet is not the most perfect secondary source for the reasons noted above, it probably would prove sufficient to generate at least one citation to something of relevance from which the known authority search technique could spring. Google Scholar provides a particularly useful alternative.

A. Google Scholar

Google Scholar is the search engine equivalent to the tiny railroad steam engine that prevails over great odds in the children's book, *The Little Engine That Could*. The product of a small staff at Google headquarters, Google Scholar aims to be the people's Westlaw or Lexis, providing searchable legal content to the general public at no cost. It does what it does extremely well – so well, in fact, that a keyword search in Google Scholar often produces results that are remarkably similar to those of equivalent searches in the basic legal databases of its fee-based competitors. Accordingly, Google Scholar has become the legal research tool of first choice, not only for the layperson, but also for many savvy and cost-conscious legal professionals.

When one must resort to a keyword search, Google Scholar functions particularly well as an initial testing ground for the viability of potential key search terms. Google Scholar allows the researcher to try out *and* read the results of different searches at no cost to the client other than that of the time spent. Frequently, the researcher finds relevant materials (along with references to others). The resulting citations can then serve as the basis of economical research in the fee-based providers with their greater functionalities. The one caveat derives from Google Scholar's database. In order to provide free access, Google Scholar necessarily limits its scope to state and federal court opinions and other materials generally available on the web. Thus, while Google Scholar functions well within those parameters, it proves less useful when one's legal needs extend beyond its basic scope.

1. Using Google Scholar

To use Google Scholar:

1. Go to http://scholar.google.com/ or google "Google Scholar."

2. To search case law, click on the circle preceding Case law.

3. Click Select courts.

4. From the resulting menu of state and federal courts, check the boxes of the courts to be searched. Multiple boxes may be checked.

5. Click Done at the bottom of the menu screen.

6. Click the downward arrow at the right of the general search box to access the advanced search template.

7. Type the keywords in the applicable boxes reserved for words that must, may, or must not appear in the results as well for exact phrases. Specify a date range if desired.

8. Click the blue magnifying glass at the lower left of the advanced search box to run the search.

9. Click on a search result to pull up the text of the case.

10. Click on case citations (in blue) cited within the case to bring up the text of those cases.

11. Click the How Cited link at the upper left of the screen to access a list of cases, which have cited the case. The How Cited feature is Google Scholar's limited approximation of Lexis' Shepards, Westlaw's Keycite, and Bloomberg Law's BCite citators.

B. Subject Searching in Lexis, Westlaw, and Bloomberg Law

A successful subject search in Lexis, Westlaw, Bloomberg Law and similar databases requires a list of carefully-considered keywords. The technique for generating such a list, described earlier in Step 2, should be completed before logging on to the provider. It is also vital that the researcher have a clear idea of the jurisdiction under which the issue is governed.

Most search engines allow for the use of two different methods of keyword searching: natural language and Boolean. Natural language searching can be compared to off-the-rack, ready-to-wear clothing. Although both natural language searching and off-the-rack clothing usually fit up to a point, neither takes into account the specific characteristics of the subject (the legal problem or the wearer's body). On the other hand, Boolean searching, like specially-tailored clothing, results in a fit, which is more customized to the specific situation at hand.

1. Natural Language Searching

In natural language searching, available on Lexis and Westlaw, the researcher inputs keywords into the search box. Once the researcher clicks Search, the search engine's algorithm takes over. Based on the words input and their position relative to each other, the algorithm selects the materials with the closest fit. The search results usually are ranked beginning with those having the greatest correspondence down to those with the least.

Too many novice researchers equate the apparent ease of natural language searching with thoughtlessness. As with any keyword search, the relevance of the results reflects the relevance of the search words. Accordingly, a systematic analysis of potential keywords, as described earlier in Step 2, should be performed before initiating a natural language search. The researcher should also take care to place the keywords in the natural language search in an arrangement that replicates as much as possible the way the words are likely to appear in the source materials.

Carefully thought-out natural language searches often produce useful and relevant results. These results, however, may be somewhat generic in nature. Thus, although relevant in the general sense, the results do not always reflect the nuances of the problem being researched.

2. Boolean Searching

Boolean or "Terms and Connector" searching is an electronic search methodology that allows researchers to tailor their search results more closely to their particular needs. It is unlikely that Boolean searching entirely shuts off the underlying search algorithms of today's electronic databases. However, Boolean searching constrains the effects of those algorithms to a greater or lesser degree, depending on the configuration of the particular database. To create a Boolean search, one must first determine the keywords, or terms, that the search results must have, may have, or must not have. The keyword generation process described earlier in Step 2 of this chapter provides an excellent start. The researcher should create a list of applicable keywords and their synonyms. On this list, the researcher should include not only specific words related to the problem at hand, but also more general words that apply to the broader concepts implicated by that situation. Boolean searching is most effective when it includes the "terms of art," meaning the words typically used in connection with the analysis of a particular legal issue. Therefore, the strategic researcher, who is unfamiliar with those terms, first consults secondary sources related to the topic to look for consistently-used terminology.

The most widely-used Boolean connectors and word expanders are:

- And
- Or
- And not/But not
- Within same sentence
- Within same paragraph
- Within a specified number of words
- Exact phrase
- Root extender (allows variant endings of a specified root word), e.g. friend, friendly, friendship
- Placeholder or universal character (allows a variant letter in the middle of a word)

Westlaw, Lexis, and Bloomberg Law allow the use of all of the foregoing connectors and expanders in Boolean searching. Unfortunately, however, the three online providers have not adopted a uniform set of symbols for these connectors and expanders for application in the creation of a search. The following chart shows the iterations adopted by each provider.

Boolean Connectors in WestlawNext, Lexis Advance, & Bloomberg Law

Connectors	WestlawNext	Lexis Advance	Bloomberg Law
And	&	and	AND
Or	or	or	OR
And not/But not	but not	and not	NOT
Within same sentence	/s	w/sent	S/
Within same paragraph	/p	w/para	P/
Within a specified number of words	/[number]	/[number] or w/[number]	N/[number]
Exact phrase	" "	" "	" "
Root Extender	! or *	!	!
Placeholder	*	?	*

3. Keyword Searching Using WestlawNext

a. Initiating the subject search in WestlawNext – natural language

To initiate a subject search in WestlawNext using natural language:

1. Type the keywords in the search box. You may input a complete sentence, a question, a phrase, or simply a list of relevant words.

2. Select the jurisdiction by clicking the jurisdiction box to the right of the Search box. Click on the desired jurisdiction and click Save.

3. The home page reopens. Click Search.

b. Initiating the Subject Search in WestlawNext – Boolean Format

To initiate a subject search in WestlawNext using a Boolean format:

1. To perform a Boolean search using terms and connectors, click advanced at the far right of the search box. A list of the available connectors and expanders appears. Input your key terms with the appropriate connectors in the search box at the top.

2. Alternatively, you may click advanced at the far right of the search box and use the template at the left of the resulting screen to create a simpler (and less specifically tailored), modified Boolean search.

3. Click the jurisdiction box to the right of the search box, select the jurisdiction, and click Save.

4. The home page reopens. Click Search.

c. Evaluating the Results of a Natural Language or Boolean Subject Search in Westlaw Next

The methodology (if not the actual search results) is the same whether a natural language or Boolean search has been performed. To evaluate your results:

1. Examine the overview page that has opened. A list at the left lists the number of results by category of document — cases, statutes, regulations, secondary sources, etc. The overview — a list of key documents drawn from each category — appears at the right.

2. Review the items listed in the overview. Focus particularly on the overview listings for cases, statutes, regulations, and secondary sources. Read carefully the descriptions under each. Only click on an overview document if it is clear that it is directly on point with your issue. Remember that you will be charged for every document you open.

3. If no overview listing is directly on point, click on Secondary Sources in the left-hand list of categories and results. Carefully read the descriptions. If a number of results seem on-point, click on the result that is most directly on-point. If nothing appears relevant, click on Cases in the left-hand list of categories and results, then Statutes, and finally Regulations, until something directly on-point appears.

4. Remember that, from this point forward, WestlawNext charges for every search result you click on and open.

5. If, upon initial review of the results, the search appears relevant but is either overbroad or includes results relating to non-pertinent meanings of a search term, you can modify your search by including additional keywords and connectors in the search box at the top of the screen. If, after reviewing all of the above, it is clear the search results are off-base in terms of relevance, start over and input new search terms. However, before going forward with a second subject search, think seriously about abandoning the Westlaw search in favor of performing initial secondary source research as discussed in Step 5.

6. If a case seems directly on point, click on it to retrieve its full text. Scan it to verify its relevance, focusing on the West syllabus and headnotes. If the case is relevant, KeyCite it to verify it remains good law (as discussed in Step 6). If it remains good law, follow the procedures discussed in Step 7 to locate additional authorities from this case citation.

7. If a statute seems directly on point, click on it to retrieve its full text. Read it to verify its relevance. If it is relevant, KeyCite it to verify it remains good law (as discussed in Step 6). If it remains good law, follow the procedures discussed in Step 7 to locate additional authorities from this statutory citation.

8. If a secondary authority seems directly on point, click on it to retrieve its full text. Scan it for relevance. If the authority seems relevant, read it carefully. Note the primary authorities the source cites. Click on the citation to the primary authority that seems most on-point in terms of jurisdiction and relevance to the issue.

The primary authority will appear on the screen. Scan the authority to verify its relevance. If relevant, KeyCite the primary authority to verify it remains good law (as discussed in Step 6). If it remains good law, follow the procedures discussed in Step 7 to locate additional primary authorities from this citation.

9. Be sure to save all relevant search results in the WestlawNext folder created for this research.

4. Keyword Searching Using Westlaw Classic

a. Choosing a Database in Westlaw Classic

Although the main search screen includes a search box with an associated directory of databases, these should be avoided. The directory choices are among the largest and, correspondingly, most expensive to search. Nor are such large databases practical to search because an overwhelming number of results are often obtained. Instead:

1. Click on the View Westlaw Directory link, located in the left column of the main search screen.

2. Review the libraries described in the general directory. You want to select the smallest library that is likely to answer your question. To locate individual state materials, click on the kind of material (i.e., case, statute, etc.) in the States category. A directory of individual states appears. Click the state of your choice to proceed to a directory of its available libraries.

3. When the search screen appears, you have the choice of performing either a natural language or a Boolean terms and connectors search. Although a natural language search is simpler, it cedes greater control of the search results to the computer algorithm that

underlies the natural language search function. A Boolean search gives the researcher greater control of the search results.

b. Creating a Natural Language Search in Westlaw Classic

To create a natural language search in Westlaw Classic:

1. Type the search words in the search box. They may be input as a question, a sentence, a phrase, or simply a list of words. Try to group the words as they naturally relate to each other.

2. Click on the Thesaurus link at the right of the screen. It provides a list of words related to those you have input. Clicking on any of these words adds it to your search.

3. Click Search Westlaw.

Remember that each search conducted in Westlaw Classic incurs a charge, the magnitude of which relates to the size and/or contents of the library being searched.

c. Creating a Boolean Search in WestlawClassic

To create a Boolean search in Westlaw Classic:

1. Type the keywords in the search box, placing words and their synonyms or related terms together.

2. Click on the Thesaurus link at the right of the screen. It provides a list of words related to those you have input. Clicking on any of these words adds it to your search next to its related word.

3. Determine the parameters of the search through the placement of Boolean connectors between your

keywords to specify the combinations of words and their relative placement that must appear in your search results. A list of the available connectors appears at the bottom of the search screen. Place your cursor between the terms where the connector should appear; then click on the desired connector and it will be placed in the search box in the desired place. Alternatively, you may add the connectors manually. The list of connectors at the bottom of the screen also includes expanders. These allow you to include in your search variants of a term.

4. Click Search Westlaw.

Remember that each search conducted in Westlaw Classic incurs a charge, the magnitude of which relates to the size and/or contents of the library being searched.

d. Analyzing Search Results in Westlaw Classic

Analyze your search results thoroughly:

1. Upon clicking Search Westlaw, a list of search results appears. Related secondary source materials are noted in the ResultsPlus column at the right of the screen.

2. The search results are confined to the type of materials in the Library chosen to search. If a different type of material is also desired, an equivalent search must be run in a different library.

3. If, upon initial review of the results, the search appears relevant, but is either overbroad or includes results relating to non-pertinent meanings of a search term, click on Locate in Result at the upper right of the screen. This allows further filtering of the results with additional

key terms. Note that this refinement of the initial search incurs no charge.

4. Remember that, in Westlaw Classic *only*, no charge results from clicking on a search result.

5. If a case seems directly on point, click on it to retrieve its full text. Read it to verify its relevance. If it is relevant, KeyCite it to verify it remains good law (as discussed in Step 6). If it is good law, follow the procedures discussed in Step 7 to locate additional authorities from this case citation.

6. If a statute seems directly on point, click on it to retrieve its full text. Read it to verify its relevance. If relevant, KeyCite it to verify it remains good law (as discussed in Step 6). If it is good law, follow the procedures discussed in Step 7 to locate additional authorities from this statutory citation.

7. If a secondary authority seems directly on point, click on it to retrieve its full text. Read it in its entirety to verify its overall relevance. Analyze the cited authorities for relevance. Click on the citation to the primary authority that seems most on-point in terms of jurisdiction and relevance to the issue. Read the authority to verify its relevance. If it is relevant, KeyCite it to verify it remains good law (as discussed in Step 6). If it is good law, follow the procedures in Step 7 to locate additional authorities from this citation.

5. Keyword Searching Using Lexis Advance

a. Creating a Natural Language Search in Lexis Advance

To create a natural language search in Lexis Advance:

1. Type in the search words in the general search box on the main search page. They may be input as a question, a sentence, a phrase, or simply a list of words. Try to group the words as they naturally relate to each other.

2. Before running the search, you may further narrow it by clicking the Filters arrow at the right of the search box. You may then limit your search to a particular jurisdiction, category of material, or practice area and topic.

3. Click Search.

b. Creating a Boolean Search in Lexis Advance

Unfortunately, the tools needed to create a Boolean search in Lexis Advance are not prominently placed. This is particularly unfortunate because a Boolean search often remediates the unduly large number of results a corresponding natural language search produces.

To create a Boolean search in Lexis Advance:

1. Click on the arrow in the Filters box to the right of the main search box on the home screen.

2. On the next screen, click the Advanced Search link at the bottom of the left-hand column.

3. The resulting Advanced Search screen facilitates two kinds of Boolean searches.

4. The Search Terms function at the top of the Advanced Search screen allows users to input keywords in pre-designated categories listed on a drop-down menu: Include all these words, Include this exact word or phrase, Include one or more of these words, Exclude these words, and Include these words near each other. When the user clicks on one of these categories from the menu, a box appears in which the keywords can be typed. When the Add to Search tab is clicked, the keywords appear in the main search box with their suitable connector terms. Users can click on and fill in as many of the categories as necessary to create their search. When all of the elements of the search have been input, click the search button to the right of the main search box. The Search Terms function, although limited to the categories on its menu, generally produces a more tailored and numerically reasonable search result than a natural language search.

5. The Connectors function at the bottom of the Advanced Search screen allows users to create a Boolean search that minimizes the influence of the Lexis search algorithms to the greatest extent. This means the search results most directly reflect the user's precise needs. The user types a keyword in the main search screen and chooses a desired connector to the next word from a drop-down menu of connectors. After a connector has been selected, the Add to Search button places the connector in the main search screen. The user repeats this process with each keyword until the desired search has been created and then clicks the Search button to the right of the main search box. Alternatively, a user familiar with the connectors and their symbols may simply type the keywords and their

connectors directly into the main search screen and click Search.

6. A user may limit the Boolean search to a particular content type or jurisdiction in one of two ways. The screen with the Advanced Search link also includes jurisdictional and content restrictors. These should be activated before the Advanced Search link is clicked. Alternatively, once the Boolean search has been run, the user may use the filters at the left of the search result screen to further narrow the results by content, jurisdiction, date, additional keyword, etc.

c. Analyzing Search Results in Lexis Advance

Analyze your search results thoroughly:

1. If the researcher has not previously limited the search by jurisdiction, the researcher should do so now. Find the Jurisdiction filters in the Narrow By column at the left of the search results. Click on the appropriate jurisdiction. If the name of the jurisdiction does not appear, click on the More link to see the full range of available jurisdictions.

2. Now that the jurisdiction has been selected, one can limit the results by content type. The available content types appear at the top of the column to the left of the screen. The Snapshot link leads to a screen on which appear several of the most relevant results in all content types. Be sure to click the View More Categories tab at the bottom of the screen to see the complete range of categories. Looking at this Snapshot screen provides a good indication of the relevance of the search results.

3. If the researcher knows little about the topic of the search, he or she probably would profit most by selecting the Secondary Source content category at the beginning of the research analysis. Relevant secondary sources will explain the general contours of the topic and provide critical citations to primary source materials. If a secondary authority seems directly on point, click on it to retrieve its full text. Read it in its entirety to verify its overall relevance. Analyze the cited authorities for relevance. Click on the citation to the primary authority that seems most on-point in terms of jurisdiction and relevance to the issue. Read the authority to verify its relevance. If relevant, Shepardize it to verify it remains good law (as discussed in Step 6). If it is good law, follow the procedures in Step 7 to locate additional authorities from this citation.

4. The search results in any given content type are likely to be very large, particularly if a natural language search was employed. The researcher, therefore, must filter the results to achieve a more manageable number. Filter the results by using the prompts in the Narrow By column at the left of the search results screen. These prompts allow the researcher to limit the search results by specifying additional search terms and restricting the results to particular jurisdictions, courts, dates, attorneys and judges involved, etc. Clicking on a filter narrows the results by that delimiter. These results can, in turn, be further filtered through the prompts in the Narrow By column. Filter successively until the results sufficiently relate to your research needs.

5. If a case appears on point, click on it to retrieve its full text. Look at the Core Terms, Case Summary, Overview, Procedural Posture, and Outcome provided by the Lexis editors at the top of the document to further verify its relevance. If it is relevant, Shepardize it to verify it

remains good law (as discussed in Step 6). If it is good law, follow the procedures discussed in Step 7 to locate additional authorities from this case citation.

6. Keyword Searching in Lexis Classic

a. Choosing a Database

To choose a database in Lexis Classic:

1. Go to the Research page.

2. Look at the directory under Sources. The directory is broken into various database sets that pertain to different jurisdictions and types of materials. These database sets are known as libraries. Some include a very broad range of materials, while others are much narrower. Generally, the broader the database, the more expensive it is to search. Avoid using mega-libraries such as Federal and State Cases Combined and State Cases Combined. Opt instead for libraries that are focused to the precise kind of materials that are sought from the particular jurisdiction.

3. If federal materials are sought, click on Federal Legal – U.S. It leads to a subdirectory of the federal libraries. The libraries encompass cases, statutes, rules and regulations, various secondary sources, and other kinds of materials. Clicking on the name of the library leads to the search box where the search terms will be input. Multiple libraries can be searched together by checking the boxes that precede the libraries' names and then clicking the Search Selected box at the upper right corner of the subdirectory.

4. If state materials are sought, click on States Legal – U.S. It leads to a list of the states and territories. Clicking on the name of a state leads to a subdirectory of that state's libraries. The libraries encompass cases, statutes, rules and regulations, various secondary sources, and other kinds of materials. Clicking on the name of the library leads to the search screen where the keywords are input. Multiple libraries can be searched at once by checking the boxes that precede the libraries' names and then clicking the Search Selected box at the upper right corner of the subdirectory.

5. Broaden This Search with Additional Sources suggests secondary sources in which to search along with the primary authorities.

6. Select Search Type and Enter Search Terms is the search box itself. It allows the researcher to create either a natural language search or a terms and connector search.

b. Composing a Natural Language Search

When composing a natural language search in Lexis Classic:

1. In a "Natural Language" search, the search terms are entered without connectors. A Lexis algorithm analyzes the words and their placement and creates a list of the results that most closely match. Although a natural language search is easier to compose than its terms and connectors counterpart, it cedes control over the results to the algorithm running in the background.

2. The search terms may be input as a question, a sentence, a phrase, or simply a list of words. Try to group the words as they naturally relate to each other. Click Suggest Words for My Search to the right of the

search screen. It provides a list of alternative words for the terms you have entered.

c. Composing a Terms and Connectors Search

Terms and connectors is a so-called Boolean search. The keywords are entered, separated by various connectors, which delineate the order in which the terms must appear in the search results. The basic search connectors are listed at the bottom of the screen. Clicking on a connector in this list places it up in the search box or the connector can be typed in the search box directly. A terms and connectors search allows the researcher the greatest control over the kinds of results he or she receives.

Lexis Classic allows the researcher to refine his or her search in a number of ways, whether the initial search has been composed using Natural Language or with terms and connectors.

d. Refining Natural Language or Terms and Connector Searches

There are many options for refining searches:

1. The Suggest Terms for My Search link to the right of the search box lists additional terms that are related to the keywords input by the researcher for possible inclusion in the search.

2. The Check Spelling link checks that the search terms are spelled correctly. Spelling should always be checked because a misspelled term will impair the search results and a subsequent search to correct the error will incur additional cost.

3. The Restrict by Document Segment link allows the researcher to restrict all or part of the search to a particular part of the document as, for example, a dissenting opinion. This feature also can limit results to opinions written by a particular judge or to opinions related to cases litigated by a particular attorney. The researcher selects the segment from a drop-down list, types in the keywords that must appear in the segment, and clicks Add to incorporate the segment search in the main search box.

4. Restrict by Date limits the search to a particular date range.

e. Analyzing the Search Results

Analyze your search results thoroughly:

1. Review the search results. If they seem too broad, use Focus to search within the results using additional key terms. There is no additional charge for a Focus search.

2. If a case seems directly on point, click on it to retrieve its full text. Read it to verify its relevance. If it is relevant, Shepardize it to verify it remains good law (as discussed in Step 6). If it is good law, follow the procedures discussed in Step 7 to locate additional authorities from this case citation.

3. If a statute seems directly on point, click on it to retrieve its full text. Read it to verify its relevance. If it is relevant, Shepardize it to verify it remains good law (as discussed in Step 6). If it is good law, follow the procedures discussed in Step 7 to locate additional authorities from this statutory citation.

4. If a secondary authority seems directly on point, click on
    it to retrieve its full text. Read it in its entirety to verify
    its overall relevance. Analyze the cited authorities for
    relevance. Click on the citation to the primary authority
    that seems most on-point in terms of jurisdiction and
    relevance to the issue. Read the authority to verify its
    relevance. If it is relevant, Shepardize it to verify it
    remains good law (as discussed in Step 6). If it is good
    law, follow the procedures in Step 7 to locate additional
    authorities from this citation.

7. Keyword Searching in Bloomberg Law

As noted previously, all searching in Bloomberg Law uses
Boolean methodology.

a. Composing a Boolean Search

To compose a Boolean Search in Bloomberg Law:

1. Choose the database to be searched. Links to various
    categories of databases appear as tabs across the top of
    the homepage. The Search and Browse tab is the
    general research tab. The other tabs provide links to
    more specialized transactional, administrative law, and
    business information databases.

2. For most primary sources, click the Search & Browse
    tab. Under, Search, click All Legal Content. A list of
    content types appears. Click successively on the plus
    signs before each content type to narrow to the
    jurisdiction/scope desired. Alternatively, under Getting
    Started/Research on the home screen, click on one of

the following links: All Legal Content, Court Cases, Federal Law, or State Law.

3. Select the smallest database that suits the problem. For example, if Texas case law is required, there would be no need to conduct a search in All Legal Content, which incorporates state and federal law of all varieties. Click on the plus signs at the right of categories to access subcategories of materials within.

4. After the database has been selected, input the keywords of the search in Boolean format in the Keywords box. Click Search Help to retrieve a drop-down box of the available terms and connectors.

5. Under the Keywords box, click the Include Word Variations. If desirable, use the other filters below to limit by date, topic, industry, attorney, judge, etc.

6. Click Search.

b. Analyzing the Search Results in Bloomberg Law

To analyze your search results in Bloomberg Law:

1. Review the search results. If they seem too broad, further restrict your search by inputting additional Boolean terms and connectors in the search box at the top of the screen.

2. If the search has been performed in a database comprising various types of sources, you may limit to particular sources by checking the filters at the left of the search results.

3. The filters at the left of the screen can also be used to further narrow the results by court, date, judges and attorneys involved, etc.

4. If a case seems directly on point, click on it to retrieve its full text. Read it to verify its relevance. If it is relevant, BCite it to verify it remains good law (as discussed in Step 6). If it is good law, follow the procedures discussed in Step 7 to locate additional authorities from this case citation.

5. If a statute seems directly on point, click on it to retrieve its full text.

6. Read it to verify its relevance. Check its currency status, noted at the right of the screen. If it is good law, follow the procedures discussed in Step 7 to locate additional authorities from this statutory citation.

7. If a secondary authority seems directly on point, click on it to retrieve its full text. Read it in its entirety to verify its overall relevance. Analyze the cited authorities for relevance. Click on the citation to the primary authority that seems most on-point in terms of jurisdiction and relevance to the issue. Read the authority to verify its relevance. If it is relevant, BCite it (if it is a case) to verify it remains good law (as discussed in Step 6). If it is good law, follow the procedures in Step 7 to locate additional authorities from this citation.

Step 9: Alert the supervising attorney to unforeseen, major developments that are discovered in the course of research.

Although supervising attorneys generally neither expect nor desire a running account of the progress of your research, certain developments should be reported to them before the due date. These include:

- The discovery of anything that seriously undermines the theory under which the senior attorney and you have been working;

- The discovery of an alternative legal theory or course of action;

- The discovery of a pending court decision that will critically affect the client's case; and

- Anything that could impact the timely completion of the assignment.

Moreover, do not research issues that were not assigned to you without having first received the go-ahead from your supervisor. Other attorneys may have been asked to research those questions and any duplication of efforts will be time wasted and have to be written off.

Step 10: Stop researching when the results and the circumstances warrant.

The decision of when to stop researching will depend on the nature of the case and your budgetary and time constraints. At the very least, the most current binding authority should be consulted. When the same authorities begin appearing again and again, you can be pretty sure the field has been covered. Remember that in some, albeit thankfully rare, circumstances, the answer to the question may be that there is no answer.

Chapter 5
Statutory Interpretation Research

I. Statutory Interpretation

The legislative process by which statutes are engendered is not very conducive to clarity. Indeed, as the products of many hands, legislative horse-trading, and compromise, statutes frequently raise questions concerning their meaning and scope. Statutes may not define their terms. If terms are defined, the definitions may be ambiguous or open-ended. The clarity of statutes also can be adversely affected by their prospective nature (i.e., their applicability to situations that occur after the statute has been enacted). Unforeseen circumstances, social changes, or technological advancements often raise questions of statutory application even when a statute's language seems clear on its face and its purpose and scope is expressly enunciated.

Thus, attorneys are frequently confronted with questions of statutory interpretation. In the face of such ambiguity, a court, ultimately, must settle the question. The parties to the dispute will urge the court to adopt the statutory interpretation that is most favorable to their interests. In so doing, the parties frequently make the following kinds of arguments:

- The court should adopt the plain meaning of the disputed terms. Often that will be the dictionary meaning if the statute applies to the public generally. On the other hand, if the statute regulates a particular field, industry, practice, or the like, it might be argued that the plain meaning is the technical meaning of the term as used in that special context;

- The meaning of the terms should conform to the definition of those terms in other, related parts of the code;

- The terms, as drafted, should be construed in conformance with the usual intent of drafters who employ such a construction;

- The terms should be construed in line with the statute's purpose; and/or;

- The legislative history preceding the statute's enactment supports a particular interpretation of the terms.

It must be emphasized that the foregoing are arguments, not settled facts. Indeed, each side may employ arguments of the same type in support of the interpretation the court is urged to adopt. As noted, it will be up to the court to decide. Once it has, the meaning of the terms as they relate to the particular situation will be settled in the jurisdiction unless the court's decision is reversed or overruled. Thus, although statutory law is the initial product of legislatures, in the final analysis, it is frequently defined and refined by the judiciary.

A. Research Sources for Statutory Interpretation Arguments

Like any other kind of legal argument, a statutory interpretation argument cannot be based on opinion, but requires citation to appropriate authorities for its support. To support plain meaning arguments, attorneys cite standard dictionaries or technical manuals, depending on whether the statute is one of general or specialized applicability. The statutory code, itself, serves as the support in the context of arguments urging conformity with other enactments. Statutory interpretation arguments based on legislative history or on the drafters' construction of the terms require you, however, to resort to materials that are not so readily intuitive.

1. Legislative History

Researching legislative history requires delving into materials that were produced in the course of the legislative process as the bill made its way through the legislature prior to becoming law. The researcher seeks statements in those materials that elucidate the legislature's intent in regards to a statute's purpose, meaning, and scope. Legislative history materials fall into several basic types.

a. Committee Reports

Committee reports are generally the work of legislative staffs commissioned by a committee of the legislature to examine the likely ramifications of a proposed bill. They often explain the purpose of the legislation, the background that led to its proposal, and the arguments in favor of its adoption.

b. Committee Hearings

The transcripts of hearings of committees of the legislature often include the prepared remarks of persons who have been called to testify on behalf of or in opposition to the proposed legislation. In some cases, the hearings are more like question and answer sessions. It is not uncommon for the committee members' questions to be phrased more as policy statements than actual questions.

c. Legislators' Remarks on the Chamber Floor

The remarks of the sponsors of the bill or others closely associated with it are the most persuasive. However, the remarks of lawmakers opposed to the legislation should not be ignored. They can reveal a lot about the legislation's perceived purpose and scope.

d. Earlier Bill Drafts

When a bill has undergone a series of revisions since its initial introduction, earlier drafts can provide clues to its ultimate intent and scope. Researchers should focus on the progression of deletions and additions as the bill wended its way through the legislative process.

e. Full Text of the Enacted Bill

The statute, as it appears in the statutory code, rarely encompasses the entire text of the enacting legislation. The code typically deletes the preamble and other prefatory matter to the bill in which statements of purpose commonly appear.

f. Prior Common or Statutory Law

Inferences about legislation may be drawn from its comparison to the law it effectively replaced. Again, the researcher should pay particular attention to what was added and deleted. If the statute essentially replicates common law, judicial applications of the common law potentially could be quite persuasive.

B. Sources of Federal Legislative History – Paper

A comprehensive review of the legislative history of a particular enactment can be accomplished using paper sources.

These sources, however, are more likely to be found in law school and government law libraries than in the libraries of firms or corporate legal departments.

1. United States Code Congressional and Administrative News (U.S.C.C.A.N)

An annual publication begun in 1944, U.S.C.C.A.N. compiles in chronological order the full text of new U.S. laws, committee reports, executive orders, presidential signing statements, federal regulations, etc. A subject index and legislative tables facilitate access. Easier access is provided by the Legislative History commentary found after the text of each section of the United States Code in United States Code Annotated. This commentary provides citations to related materials in U.S.C.C.A.N.

2. CIS Annual

CIS Annual is a finding guide to legislative history materials collected on microfiche. It appears yearly in three parts:

- Index: A keyword subject index that provides the public law numbers to related bills (which can be followed up in the Legislative History part described below). It also includes legislative tables arranged by bill, report, and other numbers.

- Legislative History: Arranged by pubic law number, it provides a summary (with associated CIS microfiche reference numbers) of the reports, hearings, and other legislative history connected with the bill.

- Abstract: Arranged by CIS microfiche reference number, it summarizes the contents of each item on the microfiche set.

3. United States Statutes at Large

An annual compilation of the bills enacted each congressional session, arranged by public law number, Statutes at Large provides the complete bill text.

4. United States Congressional Record

The official record of the debates and proceedings of the United States Congress, it is published daily and divided into separate sections for the House and Senate with a keyword index. The Congressional Record is available online at: http://www.gpoaccess.gov/cri/index.html (1983-present).

C. Sources of Federal Legislative History – Electronic

1. ProQuest Congressional

ProQuest Congressional is the electronic equivalent of CIS Annual, available by subscription. Accessed by keyword or bill number, it retrieves bills, reports, hearings, transcripts from the Congressional Record, and other federal publications. Coverage depends on the subscription purchased.

2. Lexis, Westlaw, and Bloomberg Law

Legislative history coverage varies in terms of date and content; all include the Congressional Record. Bloomberg Law's legislative history content is particularly easy to access from the Legislative & Regulatory tab at the top of the home screen and the resulting drop-down box linking to a broad range of legislative resources.

D. Sources of Federal Legislative History – Internet

1. Thomas

The official site of the United States Congress, Thomas provides access to bills, lists of sponsors, votes on bills, committee reports, and Congressional Record transcripts from 1989 to the present. Note: it does not encompass hearing transcripts (but see FDSys below). Searching is by keyword or bill number. http://thomas.loc.gov/home/thomas.php

2. FDSys

FDSys, the Government Printing Office's Federal Digital System, provides keyword or citation access to an integrated group of federal databases. The advanced search function permits the search for bills, hearings, reports, the Congressional Record, and other Congressional documents. Coverage by date varies. The downside is that searches can be slow, cumbersome, and frustrating. The upside is that materials previously available electronically only by subscription are now publically accessible at no cost. http://www.gpo.gov/fdsys/

3. Statutory Interpretation Using the Canons of Construction

The Canons of construction are rules or maxims that characterize what drafters usually mean when they draft statutory language in certain ways. Although they are in no sense binding, they provide an acceptable basis for argumentation. The most widely used canons of construction include:

- *Expressio unius, exclusio alterius*: When a statute expressly states certain things are within its coverage, it excludes things that are not specifically mentioned.

- *In pari materia*: Statutes dealing with the same subject matter should be read together and assumed to share common meanings.

- Statutes in derogation of the common law should be strictly construed.

- Remedial statutes should be liberally construed.

4. Sources for Canons of Construction

The major guide to the canons of construction is *Statutes and Statutory Construction* by Norman J. Singer and J.D. Shambie Singer, St. Paul: Thomson Group, 2007-. It discusses hundreds of canons of constructions in multiple volumes.

Chapter 6
Researching Court Rules

I. Court Rules

Court rules are rules of practice and procedure that parties are required to follow when they appear in court. Some court rules apply generally throughout a particular jurisdiction, e.g., the Federal Rules of Civil Procedure or the Federal Rules of Evidence. Other court rules are localized. Such local rules include the rules of specific courts, e.g., the Rules of the United States Supreme Court. They also include the rules established by individual judges governing appearances in their courtrooms.

A. Locating Court Rules

Links to general, local, and judge's court rules appear on most court websites. Many websites include a link to Frequently Asked Questions (FAQs), which often provide additional practice tips. Practitioners should check also for links to handbooks or to guides to the rules of practice in the court. These generally provide a good summary and overview of the rules. Some include valuable checklists of required actions.

The federal government and many states have judicial websites that provide links to the component parts of the judiciary in their jurisdiction.

1. U.S.Courts.gov

Provides links to the United States Supreme Court and lower federal courts in all jurisdictions. http://www.uscourts. gov/Home.aspx

2. Texas Courts Online

Provides links to the Texas Supreme Court, Texas Court of Criminal Appeals, and Texas District Courts, along with additional links to selected lower courts. http://www. courts.state.tx.us/

3. Harris County, Texas Courts

Provides links to the county civil, criminal, and probate courts along with links to the state district courts of Harris County (civil, criminal, family, and juvenile), the Harris County justice of the peace courts, and the Houston municipal courts. http://www.ccl.hctx.net/

4. Texas Judicial System Directory

Offers an online guide to other Texas and municipal courts. http://www.courts.state.tx.us/pubs/juddir.asp

Chapter 7
Researching
Administrative Law

I. Administrative Law

Administrative law refers to the rules and regulations promulgated by the agencies of government, apart from the legislature and the courts. It also encompasses decisions the agencies make regarding the interpretation and application of those regulations, enforcement actions, and the decisions of administrative law courts operating within the agencies themselves

A. How Administrative Regulations Are Promulgated and Announced

Finding administrative law is much easier if one understands how regulations are enacted and announced to the public.

Administrative agencies are established by the legislature, which grants the agencies specified rule-making and enforcement powers. Agencies announce their proposals for rules in the jurisdiction's "register." A register is an official government publication that appears on a regular basis and reports government actions and announcements. Registers are referred to as "notice publications" because the general public is deemed to have received legal notice of any information published within them.

The announcement in the register includes the text of the proposed regulation along with a statement of the time that has been allotted for public comment. The announcement includes instructions for submitting public comment and notices of any public hearings that will be held. After considering the comments it has received, the agency publishes in the register the final text of the regulation and the date it is to go into effect.

Eventually, the new rule is published in an administrative code, which is a compendium of all of the regulations of all of the agencies in the jurisdiction, arranged by subject matter. Generally, each major subject appears in separate segments of the code called titles." The titles, in turn, are divided into progressively smaller segments called parts and sections. A keyword subject index usually appears at the end of the code.

Subsequent proposed and enacted revisions to the administrative code are referenced in a publication called a list of sections affected. The list follows the title, part, and section order of the code. If some action has been taken in regard to an existing regulation, the citation of that regulation will appear in the list of sections affected along with a page reference to the place in the register where the action was officially announced. The list of sections affected references all actions affecting regulations that occurred during the period it covers. Some issues of the list of sections affected, however, may be cumulative, i.e., incorporating actions that occurred in prior periods as well.

It should be noted that each issue of the register usually also includes one or more lists of sections affected. Researchers should check their coverage: Some may reference only regulations affected in that current issue; others may cover actions that occurred over a longer period.

B. Finding Administrative Law Generally

Keeping the terminology discussed above in mind, the researcher should:

- Perform a keyword search in the subject index to the administrative code or in a secondary source to obtain citations in the code to related regulations.

- Find and read the regulation.

- If the regulation is pertinent, go to the list of sections affected to see if its citation is listed, indicating some further action has occurred since the publication of the code.

- Find the issues of the list of sections affected that have appeared since the last revision of the code. Pay attention to the coverage of the lists as some may be cumulative. Be sure to completely cover the period from the code's last revision to the date of the last list of sections affected.

- If the regulation is listed in the list of sections affected, note the citation to the register where the action is reported. Go to the register and read the notice about the action. To bring your research up to the present date, you must also look in the issues of the register that were published after the date of the latest issue of the list of sections affected. Most issues of registers have at least one list of parts affected. Note the coverage of these lists as they may or not be cumulative.

- If the regulation is *not* listed in any of the monthly lists of sections affected, bring your research up to the present date by checking the lists of parts affected in the registers that were published after the date of the latest list of sections affected. Note their coverage as they may or may not be cumulative.

II. Federal Administrative Law

A. Sources of Federal Administrative Law – The Code – Paper

1. Code of Federal Regulations

The Code of Federal Regulations compiles the regulations of all of the federal agencies in 50 subject titles. Although published annually, code volumes appear over the course of the year in a staggered fashion in accordance with a quarterly publication schedule. This means that some volumes are always more current than others. This quarterly schedule in conjunction with the lag time for each quarter's volumes to appear necessitates the researcher's use of the List of Sections Affected in nearly every case.

The paper version has a very poor subject index. Thus, using a secondary source to find applicable code sections often saves time. Googling "Code of Federal Regulations [subject]" is another alternative. Researchers using the paper format must use the List of Sections Affected and the Federal Register (described below) to ascertain that regulations are up to date.

2. List of Sections Affected

The List of Sections Affected is a monthly publication that references actions during the month that have affected particular sections of the Code of Federal Regulations. The list follows the title, part, and section sequence of the Code and only includes citations of Code sections to which some action has occurred – e.g., a proposed revision, enacted revision, or agency interpretation. Each citation is followed by the page number in the Federal Register where the action was announced. The December, March, June, and September issues of the List of Sections Affected provide cumulative coverage to date of actions to certain titles.

3. Federal Register

The Federal Register describes itself as the "official daily publication for rules, proposed rules, and notices of Federal agencies and organizations, as well executive orders and other presidential documents." It is consecutively paginated, i.e., the pagination of each new issue begins where the previous one left off. Each issue is divided into four sections: Presidential Documents, Rules and Regulations (agency interpretations), Proposed Rules, and Notices.

A CFR Parts Affected [Month] table appears at the back of each issue. It lists in Code citation-order actions that were taken during the previous month. Researchers using paper materials should consult this table in the last issue of each month that was not covered by the most current separately-published List of Sections Affected. This more comprehensive table should not be confused with a different List of Parts Affected Table in each issue that cites sections noticed in that issue only.

B. Sources of Federal Administrative Law – The Code – Electronic

1. Lexis and Westlaw

Lexis and Westlaw provide access to the Code of Federal Regulations with coverage current to within more or less of a week. Both also include Federal Register databases, which should also be searched to catch very recent changes not yet incorporated in the Code.

Lexis's and Westlaw's excellent keyword search engines facilitate research. Their summaries in the lists of search results are drafted to make it relatively apparent whether the entry is relevant or not.

2. Bloomberg Law

Bloomberg Law shines above the other fee-based providers in terms of its coverage of primary and secondary sources pertaining to federal administrative and regulatory law. The Legislative & Regulatory tab at the top of the home screen provides direct access to this content.

3. FDSys (Federal Digital System)

The Federal Government Printing Office's online site provides free electronic access to the Code of Federal Regulations, the List of Sections Affected, and the Federal Register. Searches can be performed by keyword or citation and may be tailored to retrieve current materials or retrospective materials of a particular date in the past. Unfortunately, the descriptions in the lists of search results are not always sufficient to determine easily whether a result is relevant or not. Results can also be slow to download.

A major drawback is that the online text of the Code of Federal Regulations duplicates that of the current printed version. Thus, it does not incorporate revisions to the Code since its publication in paper. Updating, therefore, requires further searches of FDSys' List of Sections Affected and Federal Register databases. This effectively (and frustratingly) forces the researcher to duplicate electronically the cumbersome process of updating using paper sources. Although, in theory, a researcher could perform a combined search of the Code of Federal Regulations, the List of Sections Affected, and the Federal Register on FDSys, such a search would be highly unmanageable in practice, owing to the inordinate number of poorly described results it would engender.

4. Electronic Code of Federal Regulations (e-CFR)

The Electronic Code of Federal Regulations provides an antidote to the maddening impracticability of administrative law research on FDSys. This free, online version of the CFR is also maintained by the Government Printing Office. Although the GPO expressly states that it is not "an official version" of the Code, the e-CFR is invaluable because it updates the text of the Code on a daily basis to reflect the revisions made to it. A downside is that the E-CFR is searchable by citation only. http://ecfr.gpoaccess.gov/cgi/t/text/text-idx?c=ecfr&tpl=%2Findex.tpl

C. Federal Administrative Law – Agency Interpretations and Decisions of Administrative Law Courts

Agency interpretations are statements by an agency indicating how the agency will construe and/or enforce a regulation. Announcements of important policy changes and rule interpretations may be announced in the register. Rule interpretations are also announced in so-called "opinion letters." Opinion letters are published answers written by the agency to questions posed by outside individuals or entities, asking how the agency would respond if certain actions were taken.

Some agencies include a judicial branch in addition to their rule-making and enforcement arms. Enforcement proceedings are usually tried first in the agency's administrative law court presided over by an administrative law judge. Administrative law courts issue written decisions that may be found on the agencies' websites or in commercial publications or fee-based databases. When the decisions of federal administrative law courts are appealed, the cases are transferred to federal district courts, where they are retried and then proceed, if necessary, through the standard federal appellate process.

Agency interpretations and decisions of administrative law court decisions can be elusive. Notices in registers will be reported in lists of sections affected and lists of parts affected under the citations of the affected sections. Agency websites may report recent opinion letters and administrative law court decisions. Specialized secondary sources relating to agency law, e.g., the BNA and CCH publications, report some opinion letters and decisions. Lexis and Westlaw have administrative law data bases. Coverage varies and neither is a fully comprehensive source. Bloomberg Law is often a better alternative as it places special emphasis on business and regulatory sources.

D. Federal Administrative Law – Other Information

Federal agencies publish a wide range of informational materials beyond the basic rules and regulations. These include such things as public service announcements, guides, handbooks, manuals, and instructions for obtaining various forms of federal aid. The following online sites make these materials searchable and more readily available:

1. FedWorld.Gov

FedWorld.gov describes itself as "the online locator service for a comprehensive inventory of information disseminated by the Federal Government." It provides links to the principal agency websites by either name or topic. FedWorld.Gov also provides access to USASearch.gov (described below). http://fedworld.ntis.gov/

2. USASearch.gov

USASearch.gov is a search engine of over 30 million government websites with keyword search capabilities in basic and advanced modes. http://www.usa.gov/

3. GPO MetaLib

GPO MetaLib is an online search engine of government publications and materials held in government collections such as the Library of Congress. http://metalib.gpo.gov/V/LDCPLBC94F6PA8VPFGRSI2885J4F56DH7E3Q15HCYTMMKUIM9G-09434?RN=221308117&pds_handle=GUEST

4. Securities and Exchange Commission Filings

The Securities and Exchange Commission, an independent federal agency, regulates the nation's publically-traded companies. It requires these companies to make periodic filings over the course of the year that disclose such things as their balance sheets, ongoing litigation, and other information of interest to shareholders and investors. These filings are made readily available to the public on the SEC website through a searchable database called Edgar.

Edgar provides searchable access to the required filings of publically-traded companies by company name, ticker symbol, file number, etc. It also includes information relating to mutual funds. Disclosures are accessible within minutes of their electronic filing with the SEC and can be downloaded in full text. http://www.sec.gov/

III. Texas Administrative Law

A. Texas Administrative Law Sources – The Code – Paper

1. Texas Administrative Code

The Texas Administrative Code compiles the rules and regulations of all of Texas' agencies in 16 titles. Gaps in the numbering of the titles leave room for the inclusion of additional titles as warranted.

The paper version of the Code is updated by pocket parts. A keyword subject index to the Code is updated and republished annually in paperback.

Updating of the Code requires the use of TAC Titles Affected found in the Texas Register (discussed below).

2. TAC Titles Affected

The TAC Titles Affected is the Texas equivalent to the federal List of Sections Affected. It appears in each issue of the Texas Register and is cumulated quarterly. Texas Register issues incorporating the cumulative version are delineated by a different colored cover.

The TAC Titles Affected follows the arrangement of the Texas Administrative Code. Citations to affected sections are followed by the page numbers in the Texas Register where the action was announced.

3. Texas Register

The Texas Register includes proposed, adopted, withdrawn, and emergency rule actions; notices of state agency review of agency rules; governor's appointments; attorney general opinions; and miscellaneous documents such as requests for proposals. Each issue includes a TAC Titles Affected List of actions noticed in that issue. A cumulative list of TAC Titles Affected to date appears each quarter.

B. Texas Administrative Law Sources – The Code – Electronic

1. Lexis, Westlaw, and Bloomberg Law

Lexis, Westlaw, and Bloomberg Law provide access to the Texas Administrative Code as currently revised. In addition, Bloomberg Law includes content relating to Texas departments and agencies, all accessed from the Legislative & Regulatory tab located at the top of the home screen.

2. Texas Administrative Code Online

The Texas Administrative Code Online incorporates a Viewer that reproduces the current text of the code with revisions and search capabilities by keyword or rule number. Limiting features allow researchers to view the Code as it appeared at a particular date in the past. http://www.sos.state.tx.us/tac/

3. TAC Titles Affected

Its usefulness having been obviated by the availability of the continuously revised version of the Texas Administrative Code online, the TAC Titles Affected is no longer available on the web.

4. Texas Register

The online version is searchable by keyword, agency name, title number, rule number, etc. http://www.sos.state.tx.us/texreg/index.shtml

Chapter 8
Researching Nonlegal Authority

I. Nonlegal Authority

Nonlegal authorities include any kind of information that, although not the law itself, illuminates the setting in which the law operates. Attorneys use nonlegal authority to place the facts of a case in a broader context by portraying the social, political, technological, or scientific background in which the legal action arises.

II. Sources of Nonlegal Authority

A. Public Records

Public records are increasingly available online through government websites. Lexis, Westlaw, and other fee-based legal providers also have extensive public record databases.

B. Governmental Publications

Government reports, including census data, are an excellent source of statistical information. They can be found on Lexis, Westlaw, and other fee-based providers.

C. Nongovernmental Publications

Many nongovernmental publications are posted on the sponsoring organizations' websites. Google and other general internet searches, searches of online library catalogues, and searches of Amazon.com and other online book retailers often provide references to useful sources.

D. Nonlegal Periodicals and Newspapers

Google and other general internet searches frequently provide citations to periodical and newspaper articles. Many articles are accessible from the web either free or for a fee. Researchers with public library cards are sometimes able to access fee-based periodical databases from the libraries' websites without charge. Lexis, Westlaw, and Bloomberg Law also have extensive general periodical and newspaper databases.

E. Transcripts of Radio and Television Broadcasts

The websites of television and radio networks or of individual stations may offer transcripts of programming, often for a fee. Lexis and Westlaw provide access to transcripts of select programming with the added benefit that the databases are searchable by keyword, date, etc. You Tube may also prove a source of relevant material.

F. Industry Forecasts, Company Overviews, and Financial Reports

Bloomberg Law includes extensive databases of industry and company reports, sourced by its parent, Bloomberg Business and Financial News. These materials are accessed by the Companies & Markets tab located at the top of Bloomberg Law's home screen.

G. Polling Data

Check the websites of polling organizations. Polling data is often reported in newspapers and blogs. A Google or other general online search often produces related references.

Appendix

Part I
The Federal Legal System

I. Separation of Powers

The United States Constitution establishes three separate and independent branches of government: the Executive, the Legislative, and the Judicial.

The Constitution allots to the states any powers not specifically reserved for the federal government.

II. The Executive Branch

A. The President

The President is elected and may serve a maximum of two four-year terms. The President enforces the laws of the United States and proposes the legislative agenda. He or she can sign or veto bills passed by Congress. In conjunction with a bill's signing, the President may issue a signing statement, which explains the President's interpretation of the legislation's purpose and scope.

The President appoints the heads of the federal agencies, which oversee the day-to-day administration of the federal laws. The President may also issue legally-binding executive orders to the executive branch federal agencies to direct their actions.

The President nominates federal judges, subject to Senate approval.

B. The Vice President

The Vice President is chosen by and elected in tandem with the President. He or she serves as the back-up to the President and follows an agenda, usually determined by the President. The Vice President serves as the President of the U.S. Senate and retains the authority to break tie votes.

C. The President's Cabinet

Each member is selected by the President and serves at the President's pleasure as the administrator of an executive branch department, e.g., the Department of State, the Department of Defense, the Department of the Treasury, etc.

III. The Legislative Branch

A. The United States Congress

Congress meets in two-year cycles, which are called "Congresses" and numbered sequentially. The first year of the two-year Congress is called the "First Session" and the second year is called the "Second Session."

The Congress is divided into two houses: the House of Representatives and the Senate. The members of the House of Representatives are elected as an entire body every two years. The members of the Senate serve staggered six-year terms.

B. The Legislative Process

Any member of Congress can submit in their respective house a bill proposing new legislation. Typically, a bill relating to a particular subject matter will be introduced in both houses, but they need not be identical in form. A bill, which has been introduced, but not yet voted upon, is called an introduced bill.

In each house, the bill will be referred to the committee charged with overseeing legislation of related subject matter. The committee may hold hearings about the bill or cause reports to be issued regarding its ramifications. Until a majority of the committee votes to release the bill, the bill will go no further.

Upon release from committee, the bill goes to the floor of the chamber for general debate and a vote. However, even if approved by one chamber, the bill will go no further until a bill of corresponding subject matter is approved by the other chamber. A bill that has been passed by one chamber of Congress is called an engrossed bill.

The bills of corresponding subject matter that are approved in each house are often different from each other in language and content. Accordingly, a conference committee of members drawn from each house must meet to settle upon a common draft. The common draft then goes before each house for final approval. A bill passed by both chambers is called an enrolled bill. After passage, the bill then goes to the President for his or her consideration.

If the President vetoes the bill, Congress can override it if the bill receives the approval of two thirds of the members of each house.

IV. The Judicial Branch

A. Federal Trial Courts

1. The United States District Courts

The District Courts serve as the federal trial courts. They try civil and criminal cases involving questions of federal law. In these cases, the District Courts are bound by the rulings of law of the Federal Circuit Court of Appeals of the circuit in which they sit, as well as by the rulings of the U.S. Supreme Court.

The District Courts also handle civil cases involving state law when the amount in controversy exceeds $75,000 and the litigants have diversity of citizenship (i.e., are citizens of different states). In these "diversity cases," the District Courts are bound by and construe the applicable state's law. Note, however, that state courts are not bound by the District Courts' constructions of their laws and have, on occasion, repudiated them.

There are 94 District Courts. Each state has at least one District Court as do the District of Columbia, Puerto Rico, Guam, the U.S. Virgin Islands, and the Northern Mariana Islands. Texas has four District Courts, covering the Northern, Southern (including Houston), Eastern, and Western Districts.

Each case in the District Courts is presided over by a single judge, selected at random from the pool of judges who sit on the District Court. District Court judges are appointed for life by the President, subject to Senate confirmation. The number of judges assigned to each District Court varies.

2. Other United States Trial Courts

a. Federal Bankruptcy Courts

The Federal Bankruptcy Courts are divisions of the Federal District Courts. They handle all bankruptcies in the United States.

b. The Court of International Trade

The Court of International Trade is a court of nationwide jurisdiction, which addresses cases involving international trade and customs issues.

c. The United States Court of Federal Claims

The Court of Federal Claims is a court of nationwide jurisdiction over most claims for money damages against the United States. It tries disputes over federal contracts, allegations of unlawful "takings" of private property by the federal government, and a variety of other claims against the United States.

3. The Role of Federal Trial Court Judges

Trial court judges supervise pre-trial discovery and decide pre-trial motions, such as motions to dismiss and motions for summary judgment.   At trial, the judges supervise the proceedings and determine the admissibility of evidence and testimony presented. At the close of the trial, the judges charge the jury with the law. In criminal trials, the judges determine the sentence of convicted offenders.

In civil cases, when the parties agree to a "bench trial" without a jury, the trial court judges assume the jury's role as the fact-finder.

4. The Role of the Jury in Federal Trial Court

The jury resolves any disputes of fact. It then applies the facts of the case to the law as charged by the trial judge to reach a verdict.

B. Federal Intermediate Appellate Courts

1. Federal Circuit Courts of Appeals

The Circuit Courts of Appeals hear appeals of rulings handed down by the United States District Courts and the other federal trial courts. Every litigant in these trial courts has the right to appeal a decision of a Federal District Court to the Federal Circuit Court of Appeals in which circuit the District Court resides.

In addition to hearing appeals from the District Courts in their respective circuits, the Circuit Courts of Appeals hear appeals of decisions from the administrative law courts of the U.S. federal agencies.

One of the Circuit Courts of Appeals, the Federal Circuit Court of Appeals, also has nationwide jurisdiction to hear appeals in specialized cases, such as those involving patent laws and cases decided by the Court of International Trade and the Court of Federal Claims.

There are 12 regional circuits, each with a Circuit Court of Appeals. The circuits are called by their number, e.g., the First Circuit Court of Appeals, except for the Federal Circuit Court of Appeals, which is based in the District of Columbia. The Fifth Circuit Court of Appeals, based in New Orleans, covers Texas, Louisiana, and Mississippi.

A three-judge panel hears the appeal. It is randomly assigned from the roster of judges sitting on the court. The number of judges assigned to each Circuit Court of Appeals varies. Court of Appeals judges are appointed for life by the President subject to Senate confirmation.

The parties to the appeal submit written briefs to the Court of Appeals for its consideration. Parties may request an oral argument before the Court, but these requests are granted selectively. The appeal will be granted if at least two of the presiding judges rule for the appellant. The loser may petition the Court for an "en banc" review in which all of the judges on the Court reconsider and rule on the case. Such petitions are granted only in extraordinary circumstances.

2. The Role of Federal Circuit Court Judges

Circuit Court judges only consider appeals based upon supposed errors of law that district court judges made prior or during trial. Each asserted error must have been preserved for appeal by a timely objection at trial. Circuit Court judges do not hear appeals of the findings of fact at trials. However, in some instances, Circuit Court judges are permitted to draw conclusions from the facts found at trial, which may differ from the conclusions drawn by the District Court judge.

C. The U.S. Supreme Court

The Supreme Court is the final arbiter of federal statutory, common, and constitutional law. It selectively hears appeals of decisions of the Federal Circuit Courts of Appeals. It also selectively hears appeals of decisions of the highest state courts when federal law is at issue.

Nine justices serve on the Supreme Court. They are appointed by the President, subject to Senate confirmation, and hold life terms.

A petitioner seeking Supreme Court review files a petition for a writ of certiorari with the Supreme Court within 90 days of the adverse decision in the Court of Appeals. The petition states why the case merits consideration by the Supreme Court. The opponent may file a brief in opposition.

At least four justices must vote to grant the petition for a case to be heard. Only an extremely small percentage of petitions are granted. The Supreme Court generally does not state why petitions have been granted or denied. The Court's denial of a petition should not be construed as a reflection of the Court's opinion of the merits of the case or of the correctness of the decision below. Petitions are more likely to be granted if: 1) the issue is one of pressing national importance that demands quick resolution; or 2) different Circuit Courts of Appeals have reached conflicting resolutions of the issue, leading to a lack of uniformity in the application of federal law.

When the Supreme Court grants the petition for a writ of certiorari, the parties submit briefs in support of their respective positions to the Court. The parties have one final chance to plead their cases during oral argument before the full Court. At least five of the nine justices must rule in favor of an appeal for it to be granted. A decision of the U.S. Supreme Court is binding upon all jurisdictions, federal and state.

Part II
The Texas Legal System

I. The Texas Constitution

The Texas Constitution, ratified in 1876, is Texas' seventh constitution. It establishes the executive, legislative, and judicial branches. Notably, the Texas Constitution grants the state government only powers, which it specifically enumerates. Thus, unlike most constitutions, which contain general language, the language in the Texas Constitution is both highly detailed and very restrictive in terms of the powers it grants. For that reason, the Texas Constitution has been amended continuously by popular vote, making it one of the longest state constitutions in the United States.

II. The Executive Branch

Texas has a plural executive branch. Accordingly, many of the powers normally accorded to a Governor are instead dispersed amongst a variety of office holders, many of whom are elected independently of the Governor.

A. The Governor

The Governor is elected to a four-year term with no limitation of service. Unlike the U.S. President, the Governor of Texas has no authority to direct the other offices of the executive branch. The Governor, however, is authorized to call special sessions of the legislature to attend to stipulated, unfinished business.

B. The Lieutenant Governor

The Lieutenant Governor is elected independently of the Governor to a four-year term. Thus, the Lieutenant Governor does not have to belong to the Governor's party.

The Lieutenant Governor serves as a back-up to the Governor. However, unlike the Governor, the Lieutenant Governor is empowered with considerable legislative authority. The Lieutenant Governor appoints Texas Senate committees and assigns bills to them. The Lieutenant Governor casts the deciding vote in the Senate in case of a tie. In addition, the Lieutenant Governor serves as the Chair of the Legislative Budget Board and the Legislative Council. The Lieutenant Governor also plays a key role in the redistricting process.

C. The Secretary of State

The Secretary of State is appointed by the Governor to a four-year term and oversees the State's general elections.

D. The Attorney General

The Attorney General is elected to a four-year term and serves as the State's chief lawyer, primarily in civil matters. The Attorney General is empowered to issue "attorney general opinions," which consider the legality of enacted or proposed laws and agency actions. Attorney general opinions have legal effect unless overturned by the legislature or a court.

E. The Comptroller of Public Accounts

The Comptroller of Public Accounts is elected to a four-year term. The Comptroller oversees tax collection, accounting, state revenues and investments, and estimates anticipated state revenues.

F. The Commissioner of the General Land Office

Elected to a four-year term, the Commissioner of the General Land Office oversees state lands and authorizes their development and exploitation.

G. The Commissioner of Agriculture

The Commissioner of Agriculture, who is elected to a four-year term, enforces state agricultural laws.

H. Other Elected Boards and Commissions

Two of the most important elected boards and commissions are the Railroad Commission and the Board of Education.

1. The Railroad Commission

One of the most powerful elected commissions, the Railroad Commission regulates railroads, the oil and gas industries, mining, and trucking.

2. The Board of Education

The Board of Education sets guidelines for the curriculum of the public schools. Its determination of standards for textbooks carries a national reach, owing to Texas' position as a leading purchaser of primary and secondary school textbooks.

III. The Legislative Branch

A. The Texas Legislature

This Texas legislature is a bi-cameral legislature, composed of the House of Representatives and the Senate. The Legislature meets every other year in a general session unless called into special session by the governor to address a stipulated matter of unfinished legislation. The 150 House and 31 Senate members are elected concurrently to a two-year term and serve on a part-time basis.

B. The Legislative Process in Texas

Any member may submit a bill in their respective chamber. However, finance bills must be introduced in the House. The legislative process otherwise parallels that of the United States Congress.

IV. The Judicial Branch

A. Texas Trial Courts

1. The District Courts

The District Courts have original jurisdiction in all cases involving criminal felonies, divorce, title to land, election contests, civil matters where the amount in controversy is $200 or more, and any matters not subject to another trial court's jurisdiction. In large metropolitan areas, specialized district courts may be created. These specialized courts may encompass civil, criminal, juvenile, and family law courts.

The District Courts have original jurisdiction in all cases involving criminal felonies, divorce, title to land, election contests, civil matters where the amount in controversy is $200 or more, and any matters not subject to another trial court's jurisdiction.

Each District Court is bound by the holdings of the Texas Supreme Court, the Texas Court of Criminal Appeals, and the Court of Appeals of the district to which that District Court is assigned.

The geographical boundaries of the District Courts are established by the legislature. A single District Court may be assigned to multiple counties with small populations.

2. Justice of the Peace Courts

The Texas Constitution requires each county to establish one to eight Justice of the Peace precincts. Depending on the population, one or two Justice of the Peace Courts must be established in each precinct. These courts have original jurisdiction over Class C misdemeanor criminal cases. They may also try minor civil matters and function as small claims courts.

3. Municipal Courts

The Texas Legislature has created Municipal Courts in each incorporated city of the state. The Municipal Courts have exclusive jurisdiction over violations of city ordinances. They also have concurrent jurisdiction with Justice of the Peace Courts over Class C criminal misdemeanors where the penalty is a small fine. The Municipal Courts do not have jurisdiction over most civil cases.

4. Constitutional County Courts

The Texas Constitution requires each county to have one County Court presided over by a county judge. The County Courts have concurrent jurisdiction with the Justice of the Peace Courts and the District Courts over matters where the amounts in controversy are small. The Constitutional County Courts also have original jurisdiction over Class A and Class B misdemeanor criminal cases. They also serve as probate courts.

If the county has no County Court at Law, the Constitutional County Courts also serve in an appellate capacity, hearing appeals from decisions of the Justice of the Peace and Municipal Courts. In these situations, if no record of the proceedings was made in the court below, the appeal takes the form of a completely new trial.

B. Texas Intermediate Appellate Courts

1. The Courts of Appeals

The Texas Courts of Appeals hear appeals of civil and criminal cases from the District Courts to which they are assigned. The Courts of Appeals are nondiscretionary (i.e., they are obliged to hear appeals brought before them). However, these courts do not hear appeals of capital murder convictions, which go directly from the District Courts to the Court of Criminal Appeals.

There are fourteen Courts of Appeals. Each of these courts is denominated by its district number, i.e., the First Court of Appeals, etc. The Courts of Appeals sit in the following Texas cities:

First District:	Houston
Second District:	Fort Worth
Third District:	Austin
Fourth District:	San Antonio
Fifth District:	Dallas

Sixth District: Texarkana
Seventh District: Amarillo
Eighth District: El Paso
Ninth District: Beaumont
Tenth District: Waco
Eleventh District: Eastland
Twelfth District: Tyler
Thirteenth District: Corpus Christi/Edinburgh
Fourteenth District: Houston

The First and Fourteenth Courts of Appeals, both of which sit in Houston, are completely independent courts. A ruling of one is not binding on the other. Appeals are referred to one or the other by a random system. Accordingly, parties appearing in the Houston District Courts have no idea at the time of trial to which Court of Appeals their case would be referred if an appeal arises. Some confusion over the state of the law could arise at trial if the two Courts of Appeals were split on the construction of a statute or legal rule. Fortunately, such splits rarely occur.

Three to thirteen judges serve on each Court of Appeals. All are elected to six-year terms.

A panel of three judges sits for each appeal. After a decision has been rendered, a party may request rehearing. The Courts typically deny such requests. Parties may also seek an en banc review of the case by the entire sitting court. The Courts grant these requests only in unusual circumstances.

2. Constitutional County Courts

The Constitutional County Courts serve in an appellate, as well as a trial capacity, hearing appeals from decisions of the Justice of the Peace and Municipal Courts. If no record of the proceedings was made in the court below, the appeal takes the form of a completely new trial. However, in counties having a County Court at Law (see below), the County Courts take on this appellate function.

3. County Courts at Law

The legislature established the County Courts at Law in counties with large populations to assume some of the caseloads of the Constitutional County Courts. The Jurisdiction of each County Court at Law varies in accordance with the particular statute enabling it. However, in most instances, the County Courts at law act in an appellate capacity, hearing appeals from the Municipal and Justice of the Peace Courts.

C. Texas High Courts

1. The Texas Supreme Court

The Texas Supreme Court serves as the final arbiter of disputes of civil law. It has eight justices and a chief justice, all of whom are elected to staggered six-year terms with no term limits.

The Supreme Court selectively hears appeals of civil cases from the Courts of Appeals. A party seeking Supreme Court review files a "petition for review," which, prior to September 1, 1997, was called an "application for writ of error." Most requests for Supreme Court review are denied. When a request for review is denied, the Supreme Court appends a notation to its order of denial, which is referred to as the case's petition history or, in regard to denials issued prior to September 1, 1997, its writ history. Unlike the United States Supreme Court and most other states' high courts, which deny an application for review without comment upon the merits of the decision below, some of these notations provide an indication of the Texas Supreme Court's judgment of the correctness of the lower court's opinion.

Most importantly, when the Supreme Court appends the notation "petition refused" to a denial of review, the Court effectively adopts the opinion of the Court of Appeals below as its own. When this occurs, the "petition refused" notation makes the opinion binding on all Texas courts. The notation "writ refused" has the same binding effect when appended to denials of review issued from June 14, 1927 up through August 31, 1997.

2. The Texas Court of Criminal Appeals

The Texas Court of Criminal Appeals serves as the final state arbiter of criminal appeals. Eight judges and a chief judge sit on the Court, all of whom are elected to staggered six-year terms.

The Court of Criminal Appeals selectively hears appeals of criminal cases from the Courts of Appeals. However, the Court is obligated to consider appeals of capital murder convictions, which proceed directly from the District Courts.

A party seeking Court review files a "petition for discretionary review." Most requests for review are denied. The Court responds to petitions for discretionary review with petition notations. Unlike the Texas Supreme Court's notations, the Court of Criminal Appeals' notations have no precedential value and indicate nothing about the Court's judgment of the correctness of the decision under review.